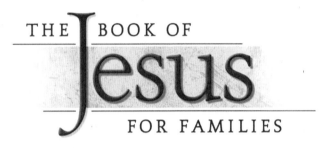

THE BOOK OF

Jesus

FOR FAMILIES

Books by

Calvin Miller

FROM BETHANY HOUSE PUBLISHERS

The Book of Jesus for Families

The Divine Symphony

Into the Depths of God

Shade

Snow

The Unchained Soul

Wind

CALVIN MILLER

THE BOOK OF Jesus FOR FAMILIES

BETHANYHOUSE
MINNEAPOLIS, MINNESOTA

Library of Congress Cataloging-in-Publication Data

The book of Jesus for families / [edited] by Calvin Miller.
        p. cm.
Includes bibliographical references.
    ISBN 0-7642-2171-X (hardback)
    1. Jesus Christ—Literary collections. I. Miller, Calvin.
PN6071.J4   B665   2002
808.8'0351—dc21

                                                                            2001005590

To Barbara

CONTENTS

TO THE PARENTS

∞

Christians have always believed that Jesus was the special friend of children. From the first time children go to church with their parents, they are taught that Jesus loves them. C. H. Woolston penned the ever popular children's lyric "Jesus loves the little children, all the children of the world."[1] J. C. Carlile wrote: *"How good to know that there is a friend for little children above the bright blue sky. . . . The love-light in his eye as he took the children into his arms has not dimmed. His attraction for the little people is unabated. Jesus delights to reveal himself to the child mind. It was not to the worldly wise and prudent, he displayed his pearls, but to those who possessed the conscious simplicity, the responsive affection of a little child. . . . Jesus was a great lover of little people."*[2] Of all the great world religions, Christ seems to have had a special place for children in the fabric of Christianity.

Jesus spoke out firmly against child abusers when he said, "It would be better for him to be thrown into the sea with a millstone tied around his neck than for him to cause one of these little ones to sin" (Luke 17:2 NIV). Both J. C. Carlile and Harry Emerson Fosdick believed that the special place Jesus gave to children in the home may have been because Jesus grew up in a house full of children.

> *Jesus' home in Nazareth was full of children—"his brothers James and Joseph and Simon and Judas" and "all his sisters"—and Jesus' understanding and appreciation of children are evident. He recalled hungry children, asking for bread or fish. He knew children's capricious moods, happy or sulky at their games. He remembered neighbors disturbing the family at midnight, when all the children were peaceably in bed. When his disciples jealously asked who among them was to be greatest, he set a child before them, saying, "Whoever humbles himself like this child, he is the greatest in the kingdom of heaven." He identified himself with children, declaring that to welcome "one such child" is to welcome him.*[3]

---

[1] C. H. Woolston, "Jesus Loves the Little Children" in *The Hymnal* (Waco: Word Music, 1986), 580.
[2] J. C. Carlile, "Portraits of Jesus Drawn by Himself" (London: Religious Tract Society, no date), 90–95.
[3] Harry Emerson Fosdick, "Jesus' Love of Children" in *Portrait of Jesus*, ed. Peter Seymour (Kansas City: Hallmark Cards, 1972), 48.

J. C. Carlile believed that even as a young carpenter Jesus made himself the friend of children, because he never considered himself too busy to take time for a crying or hurting child. This idea is not found in the Bible, but the tenderness of Christ toward all children exhibits the spirit that would have made this possible.

> Is it not permissible to think of the days when Jesus was at the carpenter's bench in Joseph's shop and to imagine that the children came to Him with their broken toys to be mended? Did the boy with tearful eyes bring the broken boat that would no longer sail upon the lake? Did the girl bring the camel without a head? What did the Master do with them? It is inconceivable that He sent them away with the sorrow of broken toys in their hearts. It became Him, as the children's Savior, to add to their pleasures just as surely as He set out to prevent their sorrows.[4]

When the theologian Karl Barth was asked about the heart of his own faith and his lifetime of study, he summed up all the volumes of his scholarship in the opening lines of a child's hymn, "Jesus loves me, this I know, For the Bible tells me so." The Christ of little children is the essence of Christian scholarship. No theologian would deny that Jesus forms the simple pier on which all of Christian theology rests.

When Jesus took up little children to bless them, he gave us the essence of his feelings about children. Every theologian has risen to the pinnacle of scholarship by passing first through childhood. Jesus made the same journey on his way to becoming an adult.

But having been both an adult and a child, he laid an astonishing truth before all Christians. Becoming a Christian can't be done by becoming adult—adults have quarreling, competitive, and hurried lifestyles. To be a Christian is rather a matter of adults becoming like little children—humble, trusting, and dependent. Jesus said, "I tell you the truth, unless you change and become like little children, you will never enter the kingdom of heaven" (Matthew 18:3 NIV). Further, all who want a Messiah who spent his time discussing theology with scholars will at last be disappointed in Jesus. He was not the sort who locked himself in a gray cell, studying stacks of old books. Jesus found himself in the center of families, enthralled by conversation and amazed by the insights of the children who surrounded him.

Let us consider the Lord of Life as he was—walking the lowly ways of earth,

---

[4]Carlile, 90–95.

gladdening the hearts of boys and girls by his smiles and by his gracious words. Some wise people have said that Jesus was always of sad countenance, that laughter never rippled across his lips. That could never have been so, or the children would not have gone near him.[5]

⁵Ibid.

TO THE CHILDREN

❧

I am so glad that your parents, or some very special friends of yours, have purchased this book. Why? Because Jesus is a special friend of mine. I am sure that he is your friend, too. It could be that you have not thought much about how very special Jesus is. If so, this book could help you spend some time thinking more about him. I hope that in doing that you will see what a wonderful life he lived and how he is not only your friend but the friend of all children who have ever lived.

Since Jesus lived on earth so long ago, he dressed quite differently from the way that you dress. He ate different kinds of food than you eat, as well. While he spoke a form of a language that is still used today, it is probably not a language that you would know. But try not to think about all the ways in which Christ was different from you. As you read through this book, look for all the ways that Jesus was like you. And you may be sure he was very much like you.

Have you ever laughed your head off at a funny story? So did Jesus. Have you ever gone to a wonderful dinner with friends? So did Jesus. Do you like to go hiking with your friends? Jesus constantly hiked—all over the countryside—with his friends. Have you ever felt hurt because someone was not very nice to you? Jesus did, as well. Do you like your mother and father? Jesus loved his parents, too. Do you like to smell flowers? Jesus did, too. In fact, he really liked wild flowers. Have you ever seen a sparrow outside your window? Well, Jesus saw many sparrows and included them in his sermons.

Oops! Did that last statement bother you? Are you thinking, *Oh yuk! I didn't know Jesus preached sermons?* He did. But relax. His sermons were never boring. The Bible—which is largely about Jesus—said that people gladly heard his sermons. They liked his sermons because they were so interesting, not at all like the sermons by some of the preachers of his day. Most of those preachers, like some in our day, were BORRRING! But not Jesus' sermons! They were interesting, full of stories. Besides, one of them, called the Sermon on the Mount, lasted only eighteen minutes. That has become the most famous sermon in history, and not just because it was short but because it had so many things to say that were wonderful to know.

You have no doubt heard how Jesus did many astounding miracles. He did most of them to help people who had a lot of pain and in some cases were dying. Jesus couldn't stand to see anyone cry. The Bible says that he cried several times himself. Most of those times he seemed to cry because someone else was feeling sad or lonely or was sick or near death.

You probably know how Jesus died. It was awful! He was killed by a lynch mob and some weak politicians. He was crucified! Nailed to a cross! That was a horrible kind of death. But one of the two who were crucified with him came to believe in Jesus even as he hung on the cross. Jesus' mother was there when he died. She just wouldn't leave him. Wasn't it nice that she stuck with Jesus even through this very hard time? Mothers are pretty much like that. It is hard to get into so much trouble that they quit on you.

If Jesus had stayed dead, nobody ever would have heard of him, and you certainly would not be reading a book like this. But he came back alive and stayed alive forever, which nobody had ever done before. Nobody has ever done that since. Why is this important? Well, you'll find out when you read the chapter called "The Big Surprise." But that's toward the end of this book, and we've a lot to find out about Jesus before that. So hang on, here we go!

I hope you will see this book as special. A lot of books have been written about Jesus. In fact, thousands. But not very many have been written for both parents and children to enjoy at the same time. That's why I wrote this book. As you and your parents read it, I hope you will learn a lot about Jesus.

Still, you could never learn it all. There have been so many good books written about Jesus that there are huge libraries full of them. But John the apostle, who wrote one of the most important and yet the shortest of these books, said, "Jesus did many things. If all of them were written down, even the whole world would not have room for all the books" (John 21:25 author's paraphrase).

—My name is Calvin Miller.
I live in Birmingham, Alabama.

"ROAD TO BETHLEHEM"
RICHARD JESSE WATSON

CHAPTER ONE

WHEN
JESUS
WAS A
LITTLE
BOY

GLORY TO GOD IN THE HIGHEST, AND ON
EARTH PEACE, GOOD WILL TOWARD MEN.

LUKE 2:14 (KJV)

Jesus was once a child just like you. And before he was a child he was a baby. There were things that happened to him while he was a baby that he could not remember when he got older. For instance, Jesus could not remember anything about being born. Can you remember the night you were born? Of course you can't. But your mother can. She will never forget that wonderful time. If you want to know anything about it, just ask her. She'll tell you in a minute. Well, maybe not in a minute. Mothers tend to go on and on about this sort of thing. She may even tell you more about it than you want to know. That's because it was a very special time to her.

Well, the same is true of Jesus. Mary could remember every last detail of that night. Perhaps that's why we have the story in the Bible. Mary remembered the night and then told it to people like Matthew and Luke, who wrote down the story of that wonderful night.

One thing for sure you can remember is your birthday. Even though you don't remember being born, you know you were. After all, you're here. Everybody who's here has been born. That's how all six billion people in the world got here. Every year you celebrate your getting here—your being born—on your birthday. You probably have even had a birthday party to celebrate the fact that you were one year older than you ever had been before.

Well, Jesus had birthdays, too! He still does. Every year at Christmas, Jesus is one year older than he's ever been before. Since he was born about two thousand years ago, he is now two thousand years old. Every December 25 the whole world throws a birthday party for Jesus. It's called Christmas. It's a wonderful party, isn't it? I'll bet you look forward to it every year. We sing a lot of songs about Jesus at Christmas. It wouldn't be all that wrong to sing "Happy Birthday" to Jesus. Many children around the world do that on the very day that they put up their Christmas tree. It's a nice birthday sort of thing to do for the most widely celebrated birthday in the world.

But on the night that Jesus was born, Mary, his mother, never thought of putting up a tree and singing "Happy Birthday" to him. She was just glad her little Jesus had been born. It all happened in Bethlehem in a little village a long, long way from your hometown. His birth was quite different from yours. He wasn't born in a hospital with a lot of doctors and nurses standing around him. He was born in a stable with animals standing around him. You have to admit that everything about his birth was quite unusual. Maybe that's why it is so fascinating to us. Maybe that's why we never get tired of hearing about it.

MARY TELLS ABOUT THE NIGHT JESUS WAS BORN

Calvin Miller

Here is a story of some of the feelings Mary had during the time she waited for Jesus to be born. Some of this is imagined, so try yourself to think of how all these things might have happened. The point is to be very sure that Jesus really was born. And we really must believe the Bible story above all.

❧

My name is Mary. You might have heard of my husband, Joseph. I'm sure you have heard of our little baby boy. His name is Jesus, and he's pretty famous now. But a long time before he became famous, he was just a little baby who was born like any other baby. Back then we had no idea how famous he would become.

Here's how the story starts.

One night a long time ago, I was sitting at home hoping that my boyfriend, Joseph, would come to see me. I loved Joseph, and we had even talked about getting married. My mother liked Joseph because he was so kind, and my father liked him because he was a carpenter and could do a lot of handyman stuff—like help fix our roof after big windstorms. I liked him because he was the best person I had ever met and because he always treated me so kindly when we walked home from synagogue together.

But on this particular night, for some reason Joseph didn't come.

Guess who did come? Gabriel.

Gabriel is an angel, and pretty famous as angels go. In fact, he is about the best-known angel in history. But famous or not, angels can be pretty scary. In the first place, they usually just show up all at once—when you're not expecting them. This wouldn't be too bad if they were normal sized, but they're awfully big and very shiny. Gabriel didn't mean to scare me, and when he realized how badly he had frightened me, he seemed apologetic.

"Don't be afraid, Mary," he said.

I know he meant well, but I was scared to death. My heart was pounding and my knees were knocking together.

"Mary, you are going to have a baby," said Gabriel. "Joseph will not be the baby's father."

"Then who will be? I don't know any other men!"

"The Holy Spirit!"

"How can the Holy Spirit be a father?"

"All things are possible with God, Mary."

"I guess so."

Then Gabriel left. I was glad. I found him pretty hard to talk to.

But once you've seen an angel, you're edgy for a while. It was hard for me to sleep the next few nights, just thinking he might pop in and scare me to death and then once again tell me not to be afraid.

Well, the angel was right. It wasn't long before I could tell I was going to be a mother. I knew everyone would soon ask how I was feeling and who was going to be the father. I decided to tell Joseph about it.

"That's crazy!" said Joseph. "Men are the fathers of babies, not God!"

"Well, not my baby!" I said.

"I'll have to think about this!" said Joseph.

He did.

Then he came back and said, "I'm sorry, Mary. I just don't believe you. I can't think of a single baby that has ever been born without a father, can you?"

I thought and thought, but I couldn't think of one, either.

"No, Joseph, I can't. Of course, that's how God works most of the time. He usually does very unbelievable things only once! Can you think of anybody but Moses who ever split the Red Sea?"

"No, Mary, I can't."

"Me neither. So there you are, Joseph. If Moses is the only one who ever split the

Red Sea, maybe I'll be the only one who ever has a baby without an ordinary man being the baby's father."

"I'll have to think about this!"

He did.

Then he came back to me. "Mary, I just hate to tell you this, but I can't marry you after all. I don't believe you, and I don't think anyone else will believe you."

"But what about the angel I saw?" I asked.

"Well, Mary, I love you, but I don't believe you saw an angel, either."

I cried when Joseph said that. Usually when I cried, Joseph would put his arm around me and say, "Now, now, Mary. Don't cry." It's not so hard to feel bad if someone's there to say, "Now, now, dearie." But when there's no one there to say it, you can feel *very* bad. So this time when Joseph just walked away I really felt like crying.

I have always believed when you feel bad, you should try to tell God, because he can either make you feel better or he can show you why feeling bad is all right under the circumstances. So I prayed, "Dear God, I wish Joseph believed in angels."

It seemed like I could almost hear God say out loud, "He will very shortly!"

Well, that very night, when Joseph was sleeping, Gabriel came to him.

"Ta-da!" Gabriel said, surprising Joseph and causing him suddenly to believe in angels. "Joseph! You better go ahead and marry Mary. When her baby is born, you will name him Jesus. He will be the Savior and will save his people from their sins."

When Joseph woke up, he was covered with sweat.

He ran over to my house as fast as his sandals would carry him.

"Mary, I have seen the very same angel you saw!"

"Glory be to God!" I shouted.

"Mary, let's get married right now!"

"Well, I think we should wait till tomorrow afternoon so we can invite a few friends."

And so we did.

One day, after we'd been married for several months, Joseph said, "Mary, I got a notice. We have to go to Bethlehem to pay our taxes."

"Joseph," I said, "we can't take this trip. Our baby is due any day."

"Mary, the Romans will arrest us if we don't take this tax trip. We gotta go pay our taxes."

I realized he was right.

We owned a little donkey, and Joseph had made a little sidesaddle in his carpenter's shop. It was so close to the baby's time to be born that I needed to ride for part of the journey. Bethlehem was more than fifty miles away. The baby was so close to being born that my stomach stuck out quite a ways, which made my back really hurt.

"Joseph, my back hurts," I said, and I wanted to cry.

"Now, now, Mary, don't cry," he said as he patted me and hugged me. He was so kind, and it surprised me that I heard him say under his breath, "Grrrr. Romans!"

I think it was the only time I ever heard him growl at the Romans. Lucky for us there weren't any around at the time.

We traveled for days. I was so glad when I could see the walls and towers of Jerusalem rising in the distance. We walked past Jerusalem in the early afternoon and finally came to Bethlehem about dark.

"Joseph," I said, "I think I'm about to give birth to a baby."

"Not now, Mary, please!" Joseph begged. "Wait till later!"

"Well, how much later?"

"A lot later," said Joseph.

"I'll try, but I have a feeling this baby will be born tonight."

"Well, I'll get us a room as soon as we get into Bethlehem. Maybe you'll feel better when you have lain down a little while," said Joseph.

That sounded so good! I was really looking forward to a good night's sleep in one of the wonderful little inns in Bethlehem. Was I ever in for a surprise. Would you believe that there were so many people in town to pay their taxes that there was not a single room to be found anywhere in the city?

I had never seen Joseph cry. And he didn't really cry that night. But I could see tears swimming in the corners of his eyes when the last innkeeper promptly rejected us, telling us there was no room in the inn. Still, the innkeeper told us he had a stable and that there was some nice soft straw where I could lie down. Joseph thanked him and took me out back of the inn to the stable. We went into the stable. It didn't smell all that great, what with the animals being inside. But there was a lot of straw, and it was soft. To be honest, my back ached so badly that I was grateful for the straw.

When I had been lying down for just a little while, I could tell the baby was about to be born. "Here comes our baby!" I said to Joseph.

"Well, okay! But call his name *Jesus* like the angel said."

"All right, dear," I said just as Jesus was being born.

I had some pain, but it went away real fast when I saw our little boy. I was so happy, I could almost hear the angels singing.

Actually, they really were singing in the fields just outside of town. There were a whole bunch of shepherds out there looking after sheep, pretty much like they always did, when *wham!* A whole sky full of angels scared them half to death. Then, when they were all shuddering in fear, guess what the angels said? "Fear not!" But once again, they said it so late those poor shepherds were nearly witless.

Then, while the poor shepherds were quaking in their sandals, the angels told them to come into Bethlehem and find our new baby boy, Jesus, for he was the Savior.

I couldn't help but wonder why the angels told those shepherds that Jesus had been born. In a way I wished they had told some of the older women in the synagogue, who sometimes brought food and blankets to people with new babies. But for some reason the angels just told these fieldhands. So here they came. They didn't bring any gifts or anything like that. Still, in a way they brought something better than food or clothes. They came and worshipped our little baby. It seemed funny in some ways, because people don't usually worship babies, but in this case they did. And suddenly in front of these shepherds, I remembered that our baby was God's son, the most special baby ever born.

The shepherds left.

Joseph hugged me, and we both spent a lot of time just staring at Jesus. He was so beautiful, and God had been so good to give us such a wonderful little son. Joseph was holding him and looking down at him and saying, "You know, Mary, I can hardly wait till he gets big enough to run races with the other boys in the synagogue. I'll bet he beats them all."

"Uh-huh!" I said smiling. "But he could get hurt playing sports."

"Well, maybe," said Joseph. "But we shouldn't keep him inside too much, Mary. I don't want him to be pale and sickly. Let him play outside."

"All right," I said. "But I want him to have good manners and say please and thank you and tell the rabbi he's preached a good sermon."

"But only when the rabbi does preach a good sermon. We want the boy to be honest, don't we?"

"Of course," I said.

"Know what I'm going to do, Mary?"

"No, Joseph, what are you going to do?"

"I'm going to make a carpenter out of this boy."

"Well, don't let him cut himself on the saw or hit his hand with the hammer."

"Now, Mary, you're already being too protective with the boy, and he's not a week old yet."

"Well, you've already made a carpenter out of him, and he can't even hold a hammer!"

It was our first conversation on how to raise kids. We both broke into laughter when we realized how very much both of us had to learn.

In a few days Joseph had paid our taxes. Now there were fewer people staying in Bethlehem, so we were able to move out of the stable. I felt better living in a place that was cleaner. Jesus was eating well and sleeping most of the night.

We decided to stay in Bethlehem for a while. Jesus was really growing, but I would never forget the wonderful night he was born and all that had happened. I never saw any more angels after that, so life settled down a lot. In time Jesus became a carpenter like his father Joseph. He was a very good carpenter, but then, you'd expect a mother to think that, wouldn't you?

BRING A TORCH, JEANNETTE, ISABELLA

Author Unknown

This traditional carol reflects the sentiments of children everywhere and in all ages. Very little is known about this song. It is sometimes attributed to Nicholas Saboly, but it is more likely of folk origin. It probably originated in Provence, France, in the seventeenth century.

Bring a torch, Jeannette, Isabella,
Bring a torch, come swiftly and run.
Christ is born, tell the folk of the village,
Jesus is sleeping in His cradle.
Ah, ah, beautiful is the Mother,
Ah, ah, beautiful is her Son.

Hasten now, good folk of the village,
Hasten now, the Christ Child to see.
You will find Him asleep in the manger,
Quietly come and whisper softly,
Hush, hush, peacefully now He slumbers,
Hush, hush, peacefully now He sleeps.

THE HOLY BIRTH

Jim Bishop

Have you ever wondered how Joseph reacted upon first seeing the baby Jesus? Maybe it happened like this. Jim Bishop has written wonderful "one-day" books, like The Day Christ Died. *This telling is about the day Christ was born.*

❧

Joseph had run out of prayers and promises. His face was sick, his eyes listless. He looked up toward the east, and his dark eyes mirrored a strange thing: three stars, coming over the Mountains of Moab, were fused into one tremendously bright one. His eyes caught the glint of bright blue light, almost like a tiny moon, and he wondered about it and was still vaguely troubled by it when he heard a tiny, thin wail, a sound so slender that one had to listen again for it to make sure.

He wanted to rush inside at once. He got to his feet, and he moved no further. She would call him. He would wait. Joseph paced up and down, not realizing that men had done this thing for centuries before he was born, and would continue it for many centuries after he had gone.

"Joseph." It was a soft call, but he heard it. At once, he picked up the second jar of water and hurried inside. The two lamps still shed a soft glow over the stable, even though it seemed years since they had been lighted.

The first thing he noticed was his wife. Mary was sitting tailor-fashion with her back against a manger wall. Her face was clean; her hair had been brushed. There were blue hollows under her eyes. She smiled at her husband and nodded. Then she stood.

She beckoned him to come closer. Joseph, mouth agape, followed her to a little manger. It had been cleaned but, where the animals had nipped the edges of the wood, the boards were worn and splintered. In the manger were the broad bolts of white swaddling she had brought on the trip. They were doubled underneath and over the top of the baby.

Mary smiled at her husband as he bent far over to look. There, among the cloths, he saw the tiny face of an infant. This, said Joseph to himself, is the one of whom the angel spoke. He dropped to his knees beside the manger. This was the Messiah.[1]

[1]Jim Bishop, "The Holy Birth" in *The Day Christ Was Born* (New York: Harper, 1959).

AWAY IN A MANGER

James R. Murray

*Here is perhaps the world's most famous lullaby. It
can be sung to several different melodies. But
however it is sung, it should help us to remember
that Jesus was born among shepherds and common
people of little hope so all of us
could have hope unlimited.*

Away in a manger, no crib for a bed,
The little Lord Jesus laid down His sweet head.
The stars in the sky looked down where he lay,
The little Lord Jesus asleep on the hay.

The cattle are lowing, the poor Baby wakes,
But little Lord Jesus no crying He makes.
I love Thee, Lord Jesus, look down from the sky,
And stay by my cradle till morning is nigh.

Be near me, Lord Jesus, I ask Thee to stay
Close by me forever and love me I pray.
Bless all the dear children in Thy tender care,
And take us to heaven to live with Thee there.[2]

---

[2]James R. Murray, "Away in a Manger" in Calvin Miller, *The Book of Jesus* (New York: Simon & Schuster, 1996), 143.

THE BIRTH

Charles Dickens

In the nineteenth century, Charles Dickens wrote many novels, all for adults. But he also wrote, for his own grandchildren, a set of stories telling the tale of the life of Christ. This story is from that collection. As a child Charles Dickens worked long hours in a country which at that time did not protect little children from abusive labor laws. Maybe that's why—when he had grandchildren of his own—he wanted to be sure they heard the timeless stories of Christ.

M y dear children, I am very anxious that you should know something about the History of Jesus Christ. For everybody ought to know about Him. No one ever lived who was so good, so kind, so gentle, and so sorry for all people who did wrong, or were in any way, ill or miserable, as He was. And as He is now in Heaven, where we hope to go, and all to meet each other after we are dead, and there be happy always together, you never can think what a good place Heaven is, without knowing who He was and what He did.

He was born, a long, long time ago—nearly two thousand years ago—at a place called Bethlehem. His father and mother lived in a city called Nazareth, but they were forced by business to travel to Bethlehem. His father's name was Joseph, and His mother's name was Mary. And the town being very full of people, also brought there by business, there was no room for Joseph and Mary in the Inn or in any house; so they went into a stable to lodge, and in this stable Jesus Christ was born. There was no cradle or anything of that kind there, so Mary laid her pretty little boy in what is called the manger, which is the place the horses eat out of. And there He fell asleep.

While He was asleep, some shepherds who were watching sheep in the fields, saw an Angel from God, all light and beautiful, come moving over the grass towards them. At first, they were afraid and fell down and hid their faces. But it said, "There is a child born to-day in the city of Bethlehem . . . He will teach men to love one another, and not to quarrel and hurt one another; and His name will be Jesus Christ; and people will put that name in their prayers, because they will know God loves it, and will know that they should love it too." And then the Angel told the shepherds to go to that stable, and look at that little child in the manger. Which they did; and they kneeled down by it in its sleep, and said, "God bless this child!"

Now the great place of all that country was Jerusalem—just as London is the great place in England—and at Jerusalem the King lived, whose name was King Herod. Some wise men came one day, from a country a long way off in the East, and said to the King, "We have seen a star in the sky, which teaches us to know that a child is born in Bethlehem, who will live to be a man whom all people will love." When King Herod heard this, he was jealous, for he was a wicked man. But he pretended not to be, and said to the wise men, "Whereabouts is this child?" And the wise men said: "We don't know. But we think the star will show us; for the star has been moving on before us, all the way here, and is now standing still in the sky." Then Herod asked them to see if the star would show them where the child lived, and ordered them, if they found the child, to come back to him. So they went out, and the star went on, over their heads a little way before them, until it stopped over the house where the child was.

This was very wonderful, but God ordered it to be so.

When the star stopped, the wise men went in, and saw the child with Mary His mother. They loved Him very much, and gave Him some presents. Then they went away. But they did not go back to King Herod; for they thought he was jealous, though he had not said so. So they went away, by night, back into their own country. And an Angel came, and told Joseph and Mary to take the child into a country called Egypt, or Herod would kill Him. So they escaped, too, in the night—the father, the mother, and the child—and arrived there, safely.

But when this cruel Herod found that the wise men did not come back to him, and that he could not, therefore, find out where this child, Jesus Christ, lived, he called his soldiers and captains to him, and told them to go and kill all the children in his dominions that were not more than two years old. The wicked men did so. The mothers of the children ran up and down the streets with them in their arms, trying to save them, and hide them in caves and cellars, but it was of no use. The soldiers with their swords killed all the children they could find. This dreadful murder was called the Murder of the Innocents, because the little children were so innocent.

King Herod hoped that Jesus Christ was one of them. But He was not, as you know, for He had escaped safely into Egypt. And He lived there, with His father and mother, until bad King Herod died.[3]

---

[3]Charles Dickens "The Birth" in *The Life of Our Lord* (New York: Simon and Schuster, 1934), 11–16.

THE COVENTRY CAROL
Author Unknown

When Jesus was born, King Herod pretended to want to go to Bethlehem to worship him. In reality he sent his soldiers to kill all the babies in the city, hoping to kill the baby Jesus, so he would never be king, for Herod wanted to remain the king himself and for his own sons to later be king.

The Coventry Carol represents the final lullaby of all those mothers in Bethlehem whose babies were murdered. It is a slow Christmas song intended to be both a lullaby and a funeral song. The song was first sung in a Christmas pageant—a Passion Play—sung before the grand cathedral of Coventry between the year 1534 and 1584. However, the carol is believed to be even older than that.

The important thing to remember is that when we hear this song we should feel pity for all the mothers of Bethlehem whose children were killed by a wicked king who hoped to destroy Jesus. While he failed to kill Jesus, other babies were destroyed by Herod's soldiers. This is the song of the grieving mothers.

Lul-lay, Thou little tiny Child,
Bye-bye, lul-loo, lul-lay.
Lul-lay, Thou little tiny Child,
Bye-bye, lul-loo, lul-lay.

O sisters, too, how may we do
For to preserve this day?
This poor Youngling for whom we sing,
Bye-bye, lul-loo, lul-lay.

Herod the king in his raging
Charged he hath this day
His men of might, in his own sight,
All children young to slay.

Then woe is me, poor Child for Thee,
And ever morn and day,
For thy parting nor say nor sing,
Bye-bye, lul-loo, lul-lay.[4]

---

[4]Author Unknown, "The Coventry Carol" in Calvin Miller, *The Book of Jesus* (New York: Simon & Schuster, 1996), 146.

CHILD JESUS

John Oxenham

*In this selection the writer John Oxenham describes
a neighbor boy studying the child Jesus as he worked
with Joseph on a small building project. Dear
children, let this story encourage you to imagine
what it would have been like to have Jesus as your
own neighbor and friend—in the flesh and your very
same age!*

∞

Joseph and Jesus worked at our house for three days, putting up shelves and cupboards and arranging our things, and on the third day we went into it. It was very much smaller than our house at Ptolemais, but it was big enough for two of us and my mother was well pleased with it. For me, the joy of having that boy as neighbor would have more than made up for even a smaller house still.

I had worked with Jesus and his father these three days, handing them tools and fetching and carrying, and the more I saw of this boy the more I liked him. He was a clever little workman and so even-tempered that nothing ever put him out, not even when he once hit his thumb with a hammer, a blow that made his eyes water. It was really my fault again; for I had asked him something and he had looked over his shoulder to answer me.

He made a little face at me for a moment, then rubbed the thumb violently and sucked it for a time, and then went on with his work as gaily as ever.

That first night I went up on the roof with my mother to watch the sun set between the hills along the valley. There were hills all round, but they fell back towards the east and west and our house stood so high that we could see well both ways and over the white houses of the village.

Behind the house was our plot of land enclosed by a rough stone wall. There were some vines in it and two tall cypress trees, and a wide-spreading fig-tree full of big leaves and the little knobs of coming figs.

"We can grow all we need," said my mother. "But we shall have to work, little son. We are but poor folk now."

"I will work hard, Mother—" And then we heard a joyous shout below, and saw Joseph's boy bounding along the stony track that led past his house and ours along the hillside.

"He is a beautiful boy," said my mother, as we stood watching him.

And beautiful he was, with the sunset gold in his hair, and his face all alight and his eyes shining.[5]

---

[5]John Oxenham, "Child Jesus" in *The Hidden Years* (New York: Longmans, Green, 1955).

IN THE GRAY LIGHT
BEFORE SUNRISE

Henry Van Dyke

Henry Van Dyke, who wrote this story, describes Mary's friend and relative Elizabeth. The two women admit the shepherds to the stable shortly after Jesus is born. Then Van Dyke allows us to see old Simeon blessing the infant Jesus, and finally we see how the wisemen and their gifts make possible the flight into Egypt. In this story Van Dyke imagines what might have happened had Elizabeth been able to visit the holy family soon after Jesus' birth. While this story is great, we need to remember that it does not precisely follow biblical accounts.

Many stories have originated based on imagining how things might have happened. But however it all happened, let us not forget that the characters in this story are real. And in our prayers let us thank God that Jesus really was born and these were some of the many friends he had even as a baby.

❧

In the gray light before sunrise, Elizabeth talked with Mary, who was watching her baby asleep in the manger. Joseph was listening, silent and content.

"He is a splendid boy," said Elizabeth.

"Yes," said Mary.

"But not quite so big and strong as my baby John was," said Elizabeth.

"No?" said Mary.

"Yet he will be greater than my John," said Elizabeth. "There is a look of heaven on his face, as if he came from there."

"Yes," said Mary.

"What are you going to call him?" asked Elizabeth. "He surely must have a noble Jewish name."

"His name is Jesus," spoke up Joseph. "The angel I saw in my dream told me that long ago. For it is he that shall save his people from their sins."

"Yes," said Mary.

At this moment steps and voices were heard outside. There was a soft knocking on the door. Joseph opened it. Four men were standing there. They were simple peasants with sunburned faces and rough clothes, but their manners were gentle. The eldest spoke for the others.

"Sir," he said, "we are the shepherds of the sheep which are kept near-by for the Temple sacrifices. Our names are Zadok, Jotham, Shama, and Nathan; poor men, sir, but honest and well-known in the neighbourhood. We were watching our flocks last night by the towers of Migdal Eder, where one of the prophets foretold that the Messiah should first be made known. A wonderful strange thing happened to us there. May we come in and tell it—that is, if perchance there is a new-born child here wrapped in swaddling-bands and lying in a manger?"

"He is here," said Joseph. Then after a glance at Elizabeth, who smiled, he added, "Come in, shepherds, but speak softly."

They entered, stepping as lightly as they could, and looked with wonder on the young child in his quaint bed. Kneeling, they told of their vision of the first angel, with his glad tidings that the Messiah was born in the city of David, and then of the flock of many angels singing glory to God, peace on earth, good will among men. The child John looked at the shepherds with wide eyes. The baby Jesus slept. Joseph and Elizabeth were amazed at the tale of the shepherds. But Mary, still and happy, kept all these sayings, pondering them in her heart. That is a mother's way.

When the shepherds had gone, Elizabeth rose up and nursed her own child. Then she made ready to go out.

"You must have a better lodging than this," she said. "It will be days and days before you can travel. I have two cousins here who have good houses. Their guest chambers were full last night because of the crowd in Bethlehem. But today one of them will surely have room for you. I will go and see."

⊰⊱⊰⊱

Elizabeth came back before noon, with joy in her face.

"Lemuel-bar-Zillai is making his guest-room ready. Come, let us go quickly. He will be glad to entertain us."

The house was a little larger than their own in Nazareth. Master and mistress were happy to receive them with the ancient Jewish kindness; for they were not mere strangers, they were kinsfolk. Three days later the good Elizabeth, remembering that her husband was lonely in Bethcar, tramped over the hills again to her home beside the beautiful flowing fountain of Ain Karim. Joseph and Mary with the young child Jesus stayed on in the house of Lemuel, welcome guests—welcome as angels.

Old Rites With New Meaning

There were certain forms and ceremonies they had to observe according to the Jewish law. First of all, after eight days, there was the formal naming of the child and his sealing as a son of Israel by the rite handed down from the times of Abraham. Then, after thirty-one days more, Joseph and Mary must go up to the temple at Jerusalem, for the purification of the mother and her first-born son.

It was not a long journey—only five miles—and it was a happy one. They were poor, but they had money enough for the offering of the humble—a pair of turtle doves or two young pigeons. So Mary dropped her coins into the third of the trumpet-shaped openings of the treasure chests which stood in the Court of the Women. The pair of doves was offered and the priest declared that the ransom of the first-born was paid.

An old praying man named Simeon, who frequented the Temple, and an ancient prophetess named Anna, a widow who spent all her time there, saw the infant Jesus with his parents and something told them that the Messiah for whom they had long waited had come at last.

Now lettest thou thy servant depart, Lord,
According to thy word, in peace—

Quavered Simeon, holding the infant in his arms. Anna gave thanks to God, in her thin cracked voice, and spoke of the child to all her friends.

On their joyful way back to Bethlehem, Joseph and Mary passed the tomb of Rachel with its low white dome standing beside the road. A dim foreboding sorrow came over Mary's mind. She recalled the words of old Simeon in the Temple, about the sword which was to pierce through her own soul.

"I remember," she said, "there is a word in one of the prophets concerning Rachel; something about 'a voice heard in a high place, mourning and lamenting, Rachel weeping for her children because they are not.' Can this be an omen of grief for us and death for our Jesus? He is so little, and the world is so big and blind and cruel. He may perish in its ignorant crush."

"We must take good care of him, that is all," said Joseph. "He has been trusted to us. He cannot perish until his great task is done. God has promised. We are all in God's hand. We do not know how it will be worked out. We must do our part."

Visitors From Afar

The very next day there was a strange event which brought great cheer to the anxious parents, and amazement to the neighbours in Bethlehem. Down the narrow street swayed three tall, richly harnessed camels carrying three strangers in costly raiment. They halted in front of the house of Lemuel and dismounted.

They were wise men of the East, Magians from the mountains of Persia. They said that a sign in the sky had led them to do homage to a heavenly King whose coming was foretold by the book of Zoroaster, as well as by the Jewish prophets. So they let down their corded bales and brought out gifts of gold and frankincense and myrrh. Kneeling in the house, they presented their tribute to the child Jesus.

Then they returned to the country from which they came; not by way of Jerusalem, for a dream had warned them against going back to the fierce and suspicious King Herod; but by the same road which Joseph and Mary had travelled—past Jericho and up the Jordan Valley towards Babylon and the Persian highlands.

Whether the infant Jesus knew anything of this visit of the Magi, except perhaps the glitter of their gold and the sweet smell of their incense, who can tell? But doubtless his parents spoke to him about it in later years.

It was Mary's habit to hold things in memory and ponder their meaning. What might not this coming of the disciples of Zoroaster, princes from a far land, mean for her son Jesus? Was he indeed to be a light for revelation to the Gentiles, as well as the glory of his people in Israel?

Mary, devout and strict Jewess that she was, could hardly understand this idea. Yet because she was of a generous nature and loved giving, the thought entered her heart and stayed there. So it was mingled with the very food of life which her son drew from her breasts.

Home Again to Nazareth

Never in his life had Joseph the carpenter been so well-off for money as he was after the visit of the Wise Men. It was not fast wealth that they brought him, but it was enough to make him easy in mind and hopeful for the future.

First, there were the rare and precious gums of frankincense and myrrh, the surplus of which could be sold for a considerable sum. Second, there was the gold, not a huge quantity, but at least a tribute worthy to be presented by princes to the Prince. With this small capital in hand, Joseph could easily reward Lemuel for the generous entertainment he had provided, and perhaps set himself up in his trade and stay on as a carpenter in Bethlehem.

The idea appealed to him strongly, for Bethlehem was a pleasant place in a fertile region. He had made friends there, and it was near the Temple. Lemuel favoured the plan.

"There are two carpenters here already," said he, "but there is room and need for another. The town is growing. We are right on the road from Jerusalem to Egypt, where the caravans pass. They give a lot of work in repairs on pack-saddles and chariots. I know of a good place for a work-shop. You will do well to stay here."

"I think so, too," said Joseph. "There will be plenty for me to do. And though the pleasure-palace of that vile fox Herod is on the mountain top just before us, and Jerusalem is full of heathen, after all it is the center of Israel, the holy city where the true King must be lifted up and crowned."

While the two men were busy talking, Mary was silent. She was thinking of the dear, gray little house in Nazareth, the silvery olive trees in the small garden, the flowing spring under its stone arch, the friendly peace of the hills and vales of Galilee.

Did not the old rabbis say that Galilee was a better place than Judea to bring up a child? Was not that her first and dearest duty, the holy charge given to her hands? Yet of course she would do what her husband wanted; stay with him here in Bethlehem, or go with him anywhere in the wide world.

Joseph slept at noon that day, and another dream came to him—a strange, sudden dream, disquieting, full of alarm. They were great dreamers in those times, and they paid attention to their visions.

This new dream was terrifying.

An angel told of Herod's crazy design to have all the infant boys in Bethlehem killed by his soldiers, hoping thus to destroy the young child whom he feared and hated as his predicted rival for the throne. It was a madman's idea, unspeakably cruel. But what was that to a crafty lunatic who had already killed his wife, his mother-in-law, his uncle, and his own sons, Alexander, Aristobulus, and Antipater? The Jews knew Herod too well to doubt his readiness for any bloody villainy. Joseph was numb with the terror of the dream.

"Get up," said the angel, "and take the young child and his mother, and flee into Egypt, and stay there until I tell thee."

So Joseph rose quickly, and told Mary and their kind hosts the strange message that had come to him.

With part of his gold he bought a strong white ass of the famous breed of the Nile, and plenty of gear for the journey. Hasty were the preparations and the farewells.

Dark was the night when the holy family took the great south road for the distant land of the Sphinx and the Pyramids, the land where the children of Israel were once in bondage and where the ancient idols were still enthroned in their crumbling temples.

The young child who was born to overthrow them had no throne but his mother's breast. There he reigned, in peace and joy, while the strong ass bore them through the darkness towards the exile and safety.

It was the longest journey that Jesus ever took on earth.

What befell them in Egypt, and what they saw there, we do not know and can not guess.

What is certain is that the holy family stayed there until the wicked Herod died of a loathsome disease, and his son Archelaus reigned in his stead over Judea. Then Joseph made up his mind that it would be safe to go back to Judea and set up the new carpenter-shop which he had planned with his friend Lemuel.

But it was not to be so. Another dream came to him in which he was warned not to return to Bethlehem, but to go straight on to his old home in Galilee.

So Mary came again to the little gray house that she loved and the carpenter-shop in Nazareth.

There it was that the thought of Jesus had first entered Mary's heart.

So there it was that the boy lived, and was obedient to his parents. He grew strong, filled with wisdom. The grace of God was upon him; in due time he came forth from that little hill town on his great mission to serve and save the world.[6]

---

[6]Henry Van Dyke, "In the Gray Light Before Sunrise" in *A Treasury of Christmas Stories* (Wheaton, Ill.: Harold Shaw Publishers, 1993), 72–80.

"GIFT TO THE MAGI"
RICHARD JESSE WATSON

THE THREE WISE MEN

Miriam Mason

*One of the things that delights children at Christmas
is the giving of gifts. This tradition is said to be
founded on the idea that the infant Jesus received
gifts from the Magi. While we don't know for sure
that there were three wisemen, we do know that
they brought three separate gifts: gold,
frankincense, and myrrh.*

✤

Herod, the king, lived in the city of Jerusalem. He was not a kind king and most people were afraid of him. He wished to be the richest, the greatest, and the most important person in the world.

It made him angry for anybody else to be important. The idea that another might ever be king in his place was a horrible thought to him.

One day three men came riding into the city of Jerusalem. It was easy to see that they were rich men. They rode on large, handsome camels. The camels were decorated with bells of gold and silver.

The three men wore rich clothing. Their faces were noble and dignified. They looked like kings, and they also looked like very wise men or teachers.

These three rich travelers came to Herod's palace.

"Where is the new king?" they asked. One added, "We hear that a baby has been born who is to be king of the world."

This was not good news to the proud king.

"What are your names and where do you come from?" he asked haughtily.

"I am Melchior," said one.

Another said, "I am Balthazzar."

The third answered, "I am Caspar. We have journeyed here from the far east to see the new born king."

"We have come a very long way," said Melchior in his deep, slow voice.

Balthazzar added, "We were led by a great bright star which went ahead of us."

These words sounded strange to Herod. They made him shiver. He called his court together.

"I suppose you have heard about this new king?" he said to his council. "Or rather, about this new baby?"

Herod's councilmen nodded their heads.

"In our book of ancient wisdom it says that some day a king will be born in Bethlehem," said the chief adviser. "The book says he will be called Jesus, or Christ."

"Does it say he will become a great king?" asked Herod in an angry tone. His councilmen looked nervous, but again they nodded their heads.

"That is what the book of wisdom said," said the keeper of the book. His voice shook, for he was frightened. He knew Herod would be angry.

King Herod was angry. He tossed his head. His long beard wagged fiercely.

"Send those men from the east in to me," he commanded.

When the visitors came before him, Herod made his voice very friendly.

"My council tells me that the new king will be born in Bethlehem. Please go to Bethlehem and look around for the king. When you find him, let me know so that I can send fine presents to him."

The wise looking men nodded their heads. They got on their tall camels again. The golden and silver bells tinkled with a musical sound.

It was evening. Up in the sky a star became very large and very bright.

"Yonder star will guide us to the new king," said Balthazzar. "Let us follow it."

The star, which they had seen before, went ahead of the three men. It led them westward. On and on they followed. They went through fields and across rivers. They traveled in valleys and over hills.

At last the star seemed to stop. It was right over the stable behind an inn.

The three kingly travelers ordered their camels to kneel. They dismounted from the animals and went into the stable, carrying the gifts which they had brought.

In the stable sat Joseph and Mary. Near them, in a manger, was a very young baby wrapped in strips of white cloth.

The three richly dressed men went over and looked closely at the baby.

"I am an old man but I have never seen a child so beautiful," said Melchior.

He laid a bag of fine leather by the manger.

"I bring him a gift of gold, and I hope he may be king forever," said Melchior.

Then Caspar said, "This baby has a holy look about him. I bring sweet perfumes and incense. I hope he may be a great leader for the people."

Caspar placed his gift by the bag of gold.

Balthazzar knelt and laid a beautiful chest by the other gifts. It held sweet smelling ointments in silver bottles trimmed with jewels.

"I bring myrrh," he said. The myrrh had a very sweet perfume like spice, but it was very bitter. "This myrrh is both bitter and sweet as the child's life will be."

Mary and Joseph were silent, for they did not know how to answer these strange words.

Once more the grandly dressed men bowed low to the baby in the manger.

Then they left the stable.

"We have seen the young child and left our gifts," they said. "Now we will go back to our homes in the east."

"First, however, we should go back to Jerusalem and visit King Herod again," said one. "He will be waiting to hear about this child."

The three agreed to wait until morning and then go to Jerusalem with their news.

But when morning came they changed their minds. Each had had a very clear dream. It was the same dream for all three.

They dreamed that a messenger wearing a cloak made of flame came to them. The messenger spoke to them.

"Do not go back to King Herod," warned the messenger. "Herod is not friendly to this new baby. He wishes to find him and kill him. Go home by another road so you will not see Herod!"

"This is not an ordinary dream," the three men from the east decided. "This is a true warning and must be obeyed."

The three men from the east went home by another road. They did not return to Herod's palace.[7]

---

[7]Miriam E. Mason, "The Three Wisemen" in *The Baby Jesus* (New York: The Macmillan Company, 1959), 42–50.

MAKING HIS CHOICE

C. S. Woodward

Not much is known about Jesus between the time he was an infant and the time he was the grown Messiah. But C. S. Woodward envisions the young man Christ as he may have arrived at his sense of calling to go forth to preach his message of the world's salvation.

❦

It was a beautiful afternoon in early Spring. The sun was shining, the birds were singing, and all the air was full of the fresh, clean scents of the new life which was springing up everywhere. Every leaf in the hedges, and every blade of grass on the hillside, and every little flower that pushed its way through the friendly earth seemed to be joining in one common song, "We want to make the world beautiful." It was a day on which it was good to be alive.

If you had been in the little town of Nazareth that afternoon you would have seen a young man coming out of the carpenter's shop into the village street. He closed and bolted the door behind Him and made His way by a little alley between two houses on to the path which led to the hill above the town. He walked slowly, for the path was steep and He seemed to be thinking deeply as He went. His eyes were fixed upon the ground and He hardly noticed the way by which He was going. He climbed the hill for ten minutes or more and then, when He reached a level spot, He stopped and sat down upon the grass.

For a while He sat there with eyes closed and hands clasped together, as though He was praying. Then He opened His eyes and looked about Him. First He gazed down upon the town below. It was a well-known sight. There was the cottage in which He had lived all His life; just at that moment His mother came out of the door with a bucket in her hand to draw some water at the well. He remembered how, as a little boy, He had loved to run by her side with a pitcher on His shoulder to draw some water too. There was the school at which He had learned His lessons years ago. The children were just running out; lessons were over for the day and He could hear their shouts and laughter as they hurried home. Soon they would be out on the hillside, playing their games and picking the young Spring flowers. There were the houses of His friends, the men and women He had known since childhood. In every one of them He was a welcome guest, when the day's work was done and friends met to talk around the fire or at the cottage door, before they went to rest. There was the synagogue, where each Sabbath day, as far back as He could remember, He had sat to hear the reading of God's Word and joined in the prayers and praises of His house. It had sometimes happened lately that He had been asked to take part in the Services Himself; He had read from the sacred books and spoken to the people.

As He sat looking down upon the town where all His life had been spent, His mind was full of memories of the past and they were all happy memories; His mother's love, friendships with young and old, the affection of boys and girls who had gathered round the workshop door, as he drove home the nails and made the shavings fly. Everything He saw spoke to Him of home and happiness. What could anyone ask more than these? If He searched the wide world through He could never find a spot which He would love so well.

Then He looked away from the little town and His eye followed the road which led steeply down the hill towards the valley, a mile and more below. He could not trace it all the way, for it wound amongst the hills and was sometimes hidden between high banks; but He could see the spot where it joined the great high road leading to the busy world, which seemed so distant from His quiet home. It was too far off for Him to make out the travellers along the road, but He could picture those who were passing there. He had often stood by the roadside and watched them on their journeys, merchants with their camels, bearing their goods to the great city many miles away in the south; regiments of Roman soldiers marching to their camps; pilgrims making their way to Jerusalem for the great feasts. Once every year since He was a boy He had travelled along that road Himself.

He knew that along the road there were thousands whom He could help. It led to towns and villages where there were sad hearts waiting to be comforted, sufferers waiting for someone to take away their pain, men and women waiting to be taught that God was their Father and loved them very dearly. He knew that He could help them all; it was for that reason that He had come into the world. He remembered the words of the old prophet, "The Lord hath sent me to preach good tidings to the simple folk, to bind up the broken-hearted, to comfort those that mourn, to make the blind to see, the deaf to hear and the lame to walk." Many a time had he read those words and heard them read, and He knew in His heart that it was of Himself that the words were spoken. The world to which the high road led was waiting for what He had to bring to it.

But He knew also that there were other things waiting for Him along the road. There was the loss of His home and of His friends. He would have to be a wanderer, with no home of His own and sometimes with nowhere to lay His head. He would be leaving all His friends at Nazareth behind Him; it is true that He would find new ones, but new friends are never quite the same as those we have known all our lives and amongst whom we have grown up.

There were hatred and enmity waiting for Him along the road. In the great world to which it led there were cruel men who would try to hinder His work and prevent Him doing what God wanted Him to do. In Nazareth everybody loved Him, but out in the world there were many who would hate Him.

And then He knew that down the road a Cross was standing, upon which one day His body would be stretched. The men who hated Him would never rest until they had killed Him and as He sat on the hillside looking down at the great road below, He seemed to see far along it the Cross on which He would die. It was waiting for Him there.

That was what the young Man saw as He sat on the hillside that afternoon; on the one hand home and happiness and safety, on the other the world which needed Him, but which would in the end put Him to death. He had to choose between the two. Should He decide for self and comfort or for God and God's children in the world? Again He closed His eyes and clasped His hands in prayer. He was asking God to help Him to do His will. Then when Jesus' prayer was finished He rose to His feet and with a last look at the distant road, He made His way down the hill back to Nazareth. In five minutes He was at the cottage door; His mother was waiting for Him there, wondering that He had been away so long. Taking her hands in His and looking straight into her loving eyes, He gently told her that His life at home was over. "God is calling Me," He said; "I must go out into the great world to do the work for which He sent Me."[8]

---

[8]C. S. Woodward, "Making His Choice" in *Jesus Among the Children* (London: Hodder and Stoughton Limited, 1925), 32–37.

"WOMAN AT THE WELL"

CARL BLOCH

CHAPTER TWO

JESUS
AND HIS
FRIENDS

A SAMARITAN WOMAN CAME TO THE WELL
TO GET SOME WATER. JESUS SAID TO HER,
"PLEASE GIVE ME A DRINK."
JOHN 4:7 (ICB)

Jesus had many friends. He never met anybody he didn't like. Unfortunately, we don't know the names of his playmates when he was a little boy, but you may be sure he had many of them. Some of his chums may also have been named Jesus, just like he was. This was a very popular name in that day. But most of his friends were probably named things like Mary, Martha, Thomas, Peter, James, John, Andrew, and Matthew. These were also popular names when Jesus was a boy.

But we do know the names of Jesus' friends after he became a man. What were their names? You guessed it! Mary, Martha, Thomas, Peter, James, John, Andrew, and Matthew. Did he ever call them Mary, Marty, Tommy, Pete, Jimmy, Jack, Andy, and Matt? Probably. People in every time have had ways of shortening and even nicknaming their friends.

What were some of the nicknames of Jesus' friends? Well, two of those friends, James and John, were so temperamental, Jesus called them the "Sons of Thunder." Thomas got the nickname "the Twin." Peter's real name was Simon, but Jesus had given him the nickname "Peter," which means "the Rock."

One of Jesus' friends was named Levi in one language but Matthew in another language. Matthew was called a publican—not *r*epublican, just publican—which was the word for tax collector. One of Jesus' friends—in fact, one of his disciples—was named Simon Zealotes, or Simon "the guerilla fighter." Martha was so concerned about keeping a clean house that some people might have called her "Sister Clean," although we don't know that for sure.

Do you have two friends with the same name? So did Jesus. He had three friends named James. Do you have two friends named Mary? Jesus had three. Mary of Nazareth was his mother. Mary of Bethany was a friend who sometimes cooked him a wonderful meal (though her sister Martha thought she made a terrible mess in the kitchen every time she did). Then there was Mary of Magdala, whom Jesus had once forgiven of her sins.

Speaking of Mary of Magdala, you may want to know that back in Jesus' time, people were often given names according to where they were from. Martha was called Martha of Bethany. Peter was called Peter of Capernaum. Judas was called the man of Kerioth. Jesus was called Jesus of Nazareth.

Jesus' twelve very special friends were called the disciples. They went everywhere together. They camped out a lot. Judas was one of these twelve friends, but he didn't stay a friend to the end. He betrayed Jesus; that is, he told Jesus' enemies where he was camping out on the last night of his life so they could go and arrest him. The soldiers were eager to make the arrest but they didn't really know what Jesus looked like. Therefore, they really didn't know whom they should arrest. Judas led the soldiers who came to make the arrest, and told them that whomever he kissed would be Jesus. A kiss was a sign of friendship back then. Everybody did it. It was the way people greeted one another before they started shaking hands to show friendship. Jesus felt very sorry for Judas, who betrayed him. He wanted all of his friends to be true friends to the end. One of them didn't make it. That's sometimes true of our good friends. One or two of them may not stay true to the end.

But all in all, we must have friends. Friends are wonderful. Friends are the people who come to our parties and invite us to theirs. Friends help us feel good about who we are. Friends stand by us when we're really in trouble. Good friends tell us when we're off track. And best of all, friends love us. And on that basis, I can tell you this: Jesus loves you. He'll be there in the good times and the bad. He'll help you feel good about who you are. He'll stand by you when you're really in trouble. He'll tell you when you're off track. He'll be there for you.

Adults often sing a hymn called "What a Friend We Have in Jesus." It's a song that makes a lot of sense.

THE WOMAN WHOM NOBODY LIKED

Esther Freivogel

Jesus was a wonderful friend to the friendless. Those who were scorned by an unfeeling and unfriendly world came to Jesus and knew they were loved. Imagine how you would feel if you were completely abandoned. What if no one thought you were a good person or you had never done one good thing in all your life? Jesus was the friend of sinners and the soul mate of all those who faced each day without a friend.

❦

In the land where Jesus lived there was a woman who was very unhappy. She had done wrong, but even though she was sorry for her wrongdoing, people were not kind to her. Some would not speak to her; others scolded her. One of those who scolded her was a man named Simon.

"What shall I do?" cried the woman. "I'm sorry I did wrong, and I want to do good. But no one will help me."

One day, as she walked down the street, she heard some people talking about Jesus.

"He is very kind," said one.

"He is a friend even to people who have done wrong," said another.

The woman wondered about this man named Jesus. Could anyone be as kind as people said he was?

Not long after this, she saw a man sitting on a grassy hillside talking to some people. They were listening as if they did not want to miss one word he said.

"It is Jesus," said a man who stood close by.

The woman could not hear what Jesus was saying, so she went nearer. She sat down at the edge of the crowd. She listened carefully. What was Jesus saying? She was surprised at the words she heard.

Jesus was saying: "Do to others just as you want them to do to you. God the Father loves you and forgives you. So you too must love and forgive each other."

The woman smiled. Jesus' words made her happy. She wished that she could show him how happy she was.

One day she heard that Jesus was having dinner at Simon's house. She had always been afraid of Simon. He was one of the men who scolded her.

But the woman was not afraid now. She wanted more than anything else to show Jesus how happy his words had made her. So she took the most precious thing she owned—a beautiful jar of sweet-smelling perfume—and went to Simon's house.

The woman looked in at the open door. There sat Simon looking straight at her. For a moment she felt afraid again. But then she saw Jesus and remembered why she had come. She stepped bravely into the room and stood near Jesus. She began to weep—tears of sadness and tears of joy. Then she opened her beautiful jar and poured some of the sweet-smelling perfume on Jesus.

Simon frowned and was ready to scold her. He did not want her in his house. But Jesus spoke to her kindly. "All the wrongs you have done are forgiven," he said.

The woman smiled happily. Jesus had forgiven her! He was her friend! When she left Simon's house, she was ready to do good, even to the people who had been unkind to her.[1]

---

[1]Esther Freivogel, "The Woman Whom Nobody Liked" in *My Book About Jesus* (Philadelphia: Westminster Press, 1949), 32–37.

JESUS IN THE HOME
OF FRIENDS

Mable B. Fenner

*Jesus seems to have stopped by the home of Mary
and Martha and Lazarus quite often. He always
found them gracious and kind and ready to listen to
his astounding lectures on life.*

❧

One evening Jesus stopped to visit in the home of some friends. They were so glad to see him. Mary, one of the friends, brought a basin and bathed his tired, dusty feet. Martha, her sister, hurried to see that everything was ready for supper.

After a while Martha stepped to the door to find Mary. There she was sitting at Jesus' feet. He was telling her about his father in heaven. Jesus smiled and invited Martha to sit down.

"Oh, I cannot sit down just now," she said. "I am putting the supper on the table. Do you not think that Mary should help me?"

Jesus put his hand lovingly on her shoulder. "Martha," he said. "You are a careful housekeeper. That is good; but you must never be so busy that you cannot take time to hear about your heavenly father. Come now and sit down. We can eat later and Mary will help you serve."

So Martha sat down with Mary, and together they listened to Jesus tell them about their heavenly father.[2]

---

[2]Mabel B. Fenner, "Jesus in the Home of Friends" in *Stories of Jesus* (Philadelphia: Muhlenberg Press, 1952), 17.

TWELVE APOSTLES

Child's Song

This wonderful little ditty has long been sung by children to assist them in remembering the names of Jesus' disciples. It can be sung to the tune of "London Bridge." Do you know someone who plays the piano? Maybe he or she could play it for you so you could learn to sing it.

Peter, Andrew, James, and John,
Philip and Bartholomew,
Thomas, Matthew, James the Less,
Thaddaeus, Simon, Judas.

MR. FOUR FOOT THIRTEEN

Calvin Miller

Zacchaeus was a tax collector who was so short that he had to climb up a tree to see Jesus over the heads of the tall people who crowded around him when the Savior came to Jericho. This story is recorded in Luke 19:1–9. I loved this story so much, I wrote it down in the form of a poem.

Zacchaeus, Director,
The Roman inspector,
Was Jericho Judah's
Unloved tax collector.

Zacchaeus was short.
Zacchaeus was lean.
Zacchaeus was barely
Four foot thirteen.
In a very tall crowd
He couldn't be seen.

Because he was short,
Some called him a wart.
Some called him a shrimp.
Some even called him
A wee-willy wimp!
But one name they called him
Made him turn green:

He despised being called
Mr. Four Foot Thirteen!

Zacchaeus loved only
One thing—that was gold!
He'd pile it in heaps
So when he grew old,
He still would have mountains
And mountains of gold.
For when he was timid,
Gold made him feel bold.
Gold made him feel warm
When the weather was cold.
Gold seemed like a friend
He could cling to and hold.
He was lonely and friendless,
For you may be sure
If you haven't a friend,
You're really quite poor.

Zacchaeus, Director,
Would knock on each door
In Jericho Judah
And shout, rant, and roar,
"Pay me your taxes!
So what if you're poor!
So what if your children
Are hungry or frail!
You must pay your taxes.
And if you should fail,
I'll chain you tonight
In the Jericho jail!"

Sometimes a mother
Would fall down and beg
And plead as she clung
To his short stubby legs.

"It would please us, Zacchaeus,
If you could just wait
Till the first of the month.
I promise I'll pay.
Just give me two weeks.
What else can I say?"

Zacchaeus just smiled
(As they begged and they wailed)
And ordered them chained
In the Jericho jail.

One day Zacchaeus
Woke up with a chill
And a very high fever.
He knew he was ill.

He stayed sick for weeks,
And he learned very well
That all of his gold
Could not make him well.

Day after day
Not one person came.
Zacchaeus was crying,
"I guess I'm to blame!
I've treated everyone
Evil and mean.

And now that I need them
They're not on the scene!"
On Tuesday he heard
A crowd out-of-doors.
Hundreds were shouting
Their joyous roars.

"Someone is coming
To old Jericho,
Someone so special
That each one should know."
Zacchaeus was sick,
But he too ran out
To see what this uproar
Was really about.

"Jesus is coming!"
The towering crowd
Was running around him
And shouting out loud.

Zacchaeus was frantic.
"This crowd is so tall
I can't see a thing.
Oh, why was I born
Just four foot thirteen?"
He cried as he spied
A Sycamore tree.

He climbed up the tree
And called out to Jesus,
"Hey, Jesus, it's me!
I'm perched with the birds
Up here in this tree."

Then Jesus looked up!
"Zacchaeus, come down.
Come down for I say,
I'm coming, I'm coming
To your house today!"

Zacchaeus no longer
Felt sick and alone.
Zacchaeus and Jesus
Walked straight to his home.
They had a nice meal
And Zacchaeus allowed,
"Jesus, I'm glad
That I followed that crowd."
"And Jesus, because
You've been so kind to me,
I'm going to become
The best I can be."

"I'm through being heartless!
I'm through being mean!
Whatever I owe,
You'll see, I'll repay!
All that I stole or
Took wrongly away.
I'll never again
Chain the poor, weak, and frail
For one single night
In the Jericho jail."

Zacchaeus, Director,
Became a new man.
He even seemed taller.
You know what I mean?
And no one believed
He was four foot thirteen.
They loved him so much
And he had so much fun
That many now called him
Mr. Five Foot One!

You also can have
Just hundreds of friends.
Now is the perfect
Time to begin
To do unto others
Exactly as you
Would like everybody
To do unto you![3]

---

[3]Calvin Miller, Mr. *Four Foot Thirteen* (Nashville: Thomas Nelson Publishing, 1987), 32.

FRIENDS WHO WERE AFRAID

Mary Alice Jones

All of Jesus' friends promised that they would stand by him to the end. They promised they would be brave. But on the night of his arrest, they were very afraid. Imagine Jesus that very night. He had just enjoyed a great meal with his friends and even used wine and bread as a kind of "object lesson" about how he would soon die. Then they all left the large dining room together and went to a little park where they intended to spend the night. By the time they got to the little park, it was pretty late and the twelve disciples were very sleepy. Try to imagine how it was when Jesus had some important things to tell his twelve friends, and they were full of good food and the hour was late.

❧

It was dark under the old trees in the garden. The gray branches seemed strange and unfriendly. Jesus and his disciples were talking quietly. After a while, Jesus walked away from the others.

"Stay here a moment," he said, "while I go over there alone and pray."

His friends sat on a rock. They seemed to have nothing to say to one another.

It was very quiet. The disciples were very tired. They had been so worried! One by one their heads nodded. They fell asleep.

They woke with a start. Jesus was speaking to them. "Let us be going."

They scrambled up hastily, rubbing their eyes. They felt ashamed for having fallen asleep.

Suddenly the quiet garden was full of noise. Through the darkness flashed the light of many torches. Loud voices were shouting.

"It was this way, I tell you. This is the way they went!"

"They cannot be far. We will soon find them."

The disciples looked at Jesus, fear in their faces. What could this mean? Who were these men, coming with such clamor into the garden late at night? What did they want?

Jesus did not move.

A torch was held high. Its light fell upon the little group of men—Jesus and his disciples—standing under the tree.

"There he is!"

"Seize him!"

A crowd of angry men rushed forward, armed with clubs. They were the servants of the men in the city who had become enemies of Jesus. They had some soldiers with them. One of the servants lifted his club to strike. But he stopped. The others stopped. Jesus was speaking. And something in his calm voice made them all quiet for a moment.

"Whom do you seek?"

"Jesus of Nazareth."

"I am he."

Still no one moved. The voice of Jesus was stern now.

"I tell you, I am Jesus whom you seek. Why is it that you have come out against me with swords and clubs? I have been daily about your streets, teaching and helping the people, and you did nothing to stop me. But now, in the darkness, you come out against me as against a robber.

Then someone gave an order. Roughly, some men seized Jesus. They bound his hands together with ropes.

The friends of Jesus shrank back into the shadows of the trees. They were afraid. Moving quietly, they walked back into the darkness. They escaped unnoticed.

Simon Peter stopped. He looked back. Jesus was standing there, all alone, his enemies about him. No one was with him.

"I cannot leave him," Simon Peter thought to himself. "But what can I do?"

The others had run on, out of the garden, seeking some safe place. But Simon Peter turned back and followed the torches.

By and by the crowd came to the house where the soldiers had been ordered to bring Jesus. Simon Peter stayed outside in the court with servants. He kept to the shadows. He did not want anyone to know that he was a friend of Jesus.

Simon Peter could see through a window into the room where Jesus was. The men who had brought him were speaking harshly to him, making fun of his teaching. They struck him.

Simon Peter shivered. It was cold. He came closer to the fire. Suddenly, one of the servants looked at Simon Peter in the firelight.

"Look!" the servant said. "This man was with him! I saw him. This man was with Jesus."

How frightened Simon Peter was!

"I do not know what you are talking about," he shouted loudly. "I do not even know the man."

He went away from the group, trying to hide his face. But one of the serving maids saw him and called out to the others, "This man also was with Jesus!" But now Simon Peter spoke harshly and denied it. Then a third servant came up and looked at Simon Peter closely. "Indeed you are one of the followers of Jesus," she charged. "You speak just as they speak."

Then Simon Peter spoke more loudly than before. For the third time he denied that he knew Jesus. "I know not the man," he cried angrily.

This last time, as he was shouting so loudly, Simon Peter was facing the window of the room where Jesus was. Jesus turned and looked upon his friend. In the look Simon Peter saw no anger, but only love and pity.

He rushed out into the darkness. "What have I done? What have I done," he cried over and over to himself. "He was my friend. I loved him more than any friend in all the world. And to save myself I said that I did not know him. I left him there alone, with men who hated him and beat him. I am a coward."

And Simon Peter wept bitterly.

But Jesus, in the midst of those who were mistreating him, was thinking of his friend with forgiveness. He loved Peter.[4]

---

[4]Mary Alice Jones, "Friends Who Were Afraid" in *Jesus and His Friends* (Chicago: Rand McNally & Company, 1947), 67–72.

THE LONELY PRISONER

C. S. Woodward

Jesus called John the Baptist the greatest man ever born of a woman. But even great men sometimes doubt. This selection focuses on how a very great friend of Jesus doubted and then returned to strong belief.

Jesus was going forward happily with His work. He and His friends travelled about the country from place to place, telling the people about the Kingdom which he had come to set up. Wherever He went crowds flocked to see Him, partly because they wanted to hear Him preach, but more often, perhaps, because of his wonderful power of healing the sick and comforting those who were in trouble. From time to time the rulers tried to hinder his work, but they could not do very much so long as He stayed in Galilee, for all the country people loved Him. Those were happy days, while He and the young men whom He had chosen for His friends found a ready welcome in all the villages to which they came. Even Judas, who afterwards betrayed His Master, seemed devoted to Him then.

But what was happening to John the Baptist during this time? What was he doing now that the King had come, for Whom he had prepared the way? For a little while he had gone on with his preaching down by the Jordan, but he knew that his work was finished. He was only the herald whose duty it was to announce the glad tidings of One who was to come. Little by little his followers dropped away; most of them felt that they had learned all that he had to teach.

But he did not give up his work entirely. He still attacked those who were leading evil lives. One day he denounced the most powerful person in the country, King Herod, for a wicked thing which he had done. It was a bold thing to do, for Herod was strong enough to do what he liked with a man like John. He ordered him to be arrested, and thrown into prison in a fortress a long way from Jerusalem. There he was kept in a dungeon, underground; his friends were allowed to visit him, but he was never permitted to leave his prison cell.

Poor John, he had always loved the open air and the cool winds; all his life he had wandered freely over the hills, and time and again had slept under the starry sky. Now he could never feel the breeze, nor see the stars; day and night he lay in his dungeon, where the air was never fresh, and it was dark and murky on the brightest day. No wonder he grew depressed and downhearted in his imprisonment. Even the visits of his friends failed to comfort him; they could not give him back his freedom, or bring him the scent of the heather and the sound of the running streams.

He often asked them about Jesus and His work. How was the Kingdom growing? Were evil and cruelty being driven out? Was the King triumphantly defeating the forces of hatred and sin which were so strong in the world? But the answers that his friends gave him made him more sad than ever. They said that Jesus did not seem eager to fight. He had once attacked the men who were profaning God's Temple in Jerusalem. John knew of that; it had been before he was thrown into prison. But since then, so said his friends, Jesus had gone away from the city where the battle must be fought. He was spending His time amongst the villages of Galilee, preaching to country folk and healing those who were diseased. He had not begun to build the Kingdom yet.

John was a fighter; he believed that God's Kingdom could only come by force. And when he heard of the gentleness of Jesus and how He was loved by all who knew Him, he began to wonder if, after all, he had been mistaken when he said that He was to be the King. Surely a King would fight for God against all the evil which God hates. Surely a King would be in the hardest places, not in the quiet country-side. It was true that the Kingdom was to be ruled by Love, but Love must fight with cruelty before it could win the day.

And so, as day after day he lay in his dungeon, John began to doubt. He feared that his work had been wasted and his life a failure. At last he could bear it no longer, and he bade two of his friends, who had come to visit him, seek out Jesus and ask Him plainly whether He was the King or not. "If He declares that He has been sent by God I will try to believe Him, but I must hear it from Himself," said John. Away went his friends upon their errand, and John settled down to wait for their return. It was hard to be patient with such doubts and troubles in his mind.

It was a full ten days before they were back again. As soon as the guard who let them into the cell had left, John eagerly asked them what the reply of Jesus had been. And so they told their story. "We found Jesus," they said, "in a village amongst the hills. He was surrounded by a crowd of people, some of whom had brought their sick for Him to heal; there was a blind man too, and several who were lame, all waiting for Him to lay His hands on them. We went straight up to Him and gave our message, saying that you begged Him to tell you plainly if He was the King or not. At first He took no notice of us; we wondered if He had heard us speak. He just went on with the work that He was doing. Then when He had healed a few more people He turned to us and asked us to repeat our question. So we told Him again what you had said, and all the people listened for His answer. He did not answer us at all really, but only pointed to the people whom He had just been helping. 'Go and tell John what you have seen,' was what He said, 'the sick are healed, the lame are made to walk, the blind are given back their sight, and the simple folk have good news preached to them.' That is all He said, so we came away. It is plain that He does not mean to answer."

They thought that John would have been disappointed with their failure, but to their surprise his face lighted up. "Thank God," he cried, "I was right after all; He *is* the King. I had forgotten what the Prophet said about the work which the King would do, but Jesus has reminded me; I will never doubt again. I ought to have understood that God's Kingdom of love can never come by force. It is loving deeds done for simple people which will set it up."

From that day onward John was a different man. His depression left him, and he seemed almost cheerful in spite of his cruel imprisonment. He knew now that his work had not been wasted, and that his life was not a failure. God had sent him to prepare the way for the coming King. He had done what he had been sent to do. Now his task was done; but the King, whose herald he had been, was carrying on the work. He was ready now to die, when it was God's will that he should go.

It was not many weeks afterwards that one day the guards came hurriedly into his cell and roughly led him to the place of execution. He knelt down at the block, and in a moment his earthly trials were at an end; his great, brave spirit was at liberty in the presence of God, to Whose service he had devoted all his life. For him it was a welcome and a joyful release from his imprisonment, but Jesus mourned when he heard that they had killed His friend.[5]

---

[5]Woodward, "The Lonely Prisoner," 81–86.

JESUS LOVES ME

Anna B. Warner

This is perhaps the best known children's song about Jesus. Children, let us see this song as a way to know that we can trust in Jesus' love, and that Jesus wants each one of us to be his friend.

Jesus loves me! This I know,
For the Bible tells me so;
Little ones to him belong;
They are weak, but he is strong.

    Yes, Jesus loves me,
    Yes, Jesus loves me,
    Yes, Jesus loves me,
    The Bible tells me so.

Jesus loves me! He who died
Heaven's gates to open wide!
He will wash away my sins,
Let his little child come in.

    Yes, Jesus loves me,
    Yes, Jesus loves me,
    Yes, Jesus loves me,
    The Bible tells me so.

Jesus loves me! Loves me still,
Tho I'm very weak and ill;
From his shining throne on high,
Comes to watch me where I lie.

    Yes, Jesus loves me,
    Yes, Jesus loves me,
    Yes, Jesus loves me,
    The Bible tells me so.

Jesus loves me! He will stay
Close beside me all the way;
If I love him, when I die
He will take me home on high.

    Yes, Jesus loves me,
    Yes, Jesus loves me,
    Yes, Jesus loves me,
    The Bible tells me so.[6]

---

[6]Anna B. Warner, "Jesus Loves Me" (Nashville: The Baptist Hymnal, 1975), 336.

"JESUS HEALING JAIRUS'
DAUGHTER"
C. MICHAEL DUDASH

CHAPTER THREE

SOME OF THE AMAZING AND UNEXPLAINABLE THINGS JESUS DID

> THE PEOPLE BROUGHT TO JESUS ALL WHO
> HAD VARIOUS KINDS OF SICKNESS, AND LAYING
> HIS HANDS ON EACH ONE, HE HEALED THEM.
> LUKE 4:40 (NIV)

Are you fascinated by things you can't understand? Most people are. That's why magicians have always been popular. We can't figure out how they get rabbits out of their hats. Well, magicians don't do miracles, only tricks. They make us think they're doing something impossible when there really is an explanation. They don't just suddenly create the rabbit they pull out of a hat. It was there all the time. The rabbit—poor little thing—had just been squashed in a secret compartment in the bottom of the hat. Just before they do their amazing tricks, magicians usually say something like "hocus pocus" or "abracadabra." Then they go for the rabbit or they reach out and pull a pigeon out of your bonnet; that poor bird was squashed in their sleeve the whole time.

Magicians' tricks are amazing but always explainable.

If you think real hard, you can usually figure out how magicians do their tricks. But if you had been present when Jesus did his unbelievable things, you would never be able to figure out how he did it. Even if you thought as hard as you could, you could not figure it out. That's because Jesus didn't do tricks. He did miracles. He didn't say "hocus pocus" and then tell a crippled child to walk. He was God's Son, so God gave him the power to say things like "Take up your bed and walk." He said that to a paralyzed man, and the man surprised the world by getting up and rolling up his bedroll and taking off for home—walking on his own.

Jesus did three kinds of miracles. First, healings: In these miracles he actually cured people of some disease or illness. Second, wonders: Jesus also did supernatural things like walk on water or divide five loaves of bread until there was enough to feed over five thousand people. Third, exorcisms: In these miracles Jesus ordered demons who were living inside of people to leave those people and give them back a normal way of life. In every case the demons, who were making the people do weird things, went away. Then the people they left became normal.

There is one other difference between tricksters and Jesus. Magicians do their tricks just to amaze people or to make money. In fact, they sell tickets so that people can watch them get out of straitjackets inside of a locked trunk that has just been thrown in the river. They love it when people say "OOOH! How did he do that?" They will almost never tell you; if they did, then you could get a white cape just like theirs and sell tickets and do it, too. You'll find that magicians hate competition and will rarely tell anyone how they do what they do.

But Jesus didn't do his unbelievable things just to make money or amaze people. Let's take the first kind of miracles that Jesus did: the healing miracles. He did these miracles because people were so very much in need. He hated to see people who were dying or in such pain that they couldn't smile or laugh. Whenever he saw such need, something inside him hurt so bad that he just had to heal them. Jesus himself probably had gotten the flu or a bad stomachache once. He knew firsthand what it was like to feel bad and how great it was to feel good. He didn't want anyone to have to feel hurt and pain if he could stop it. So he performed miracles and left those who were hurting free of pain. He left those whose faces were twisted in pain laughing in the joy of good health.

But what about wonders, Jesus' second kind of miracles? He didn't do those to stupefy audiences, either. He did those miracles for the same kind of reasons that he healed. When he divided the five loaves to feed the five thousand, he did it because he felt bad that there were so many hungry people in the world. Jesus knew that for a little while he had stopped their hunger. Those who often went to bed hungry were very happy. For one brief shining moment there were bread and fish everywhere.

When he walked on the water, he did that because his disciples were on a boat in the middle of a storm, scared to death. Have you ever been afraid for your life? Those disciples were. So Jesus went out to be with them. When Jesus got there, they lost their fear and the storm subsided. Jesus has never liked to see anyone be alone in a storm or in the darkness. Jesus knows how terrible it is to feel afraid.

And what about the third kind of miracles—exorcisms? He didn't say "hocus pocus" and command the demons to leave people's lives while audiences cheered. He did these miracles because he loved people and wanted to help them. Jesus didn't like to see people who were so troubled in their spirits that they were depressed or insane, all because some evil powers within them had stolen all their happiness. So he commanded those evil spirits to get out of some poor person's mind and let them be happy again. The evil spirits always left. They had to. Jesus had all power. What he said, went.

Jesus didn't come to mystify people. There is no record that Jesus was ever introduced by someone in a tuxedo crying out, "AND NOW, LADIES AND GENTLEMEN, IN THE CENTER RING—THE MAN IN THE WHITE CAPE—THE STUPENDOUS, TREMENDOUS JESUS OF JERUSALEM." Rather, he came into a circle of hurting sick people, people who were lonely and afraid, and said to them, "I have come to you so you can have life, abundant and eternal." Each time he did a miracle, he was really saying to those who were changed, "Be healthy and feel good about who you are."

SIX THINGS JESUS DID WITH WATER

Calvin Miller

Some years ago I got to thinking about water and how important it is to life. Three fourths of the world is covered with it. Without water we could not live more than a day or two. But Jesus did some wonderful things with simple water. Consider these six things he did with it.

∝

One—He Was Baptized in It

Once when John was near the river,
Jesus set him all aquiver—
And nearly put him in a dither—
By saying, "John, my friend, come hither.
I want to be baptized."
But John shrunk back and then he said,
"I baptize folks, it's true, and yet
I who scrub and get them wet
Am but the sinner, Lord, it's true.
So I should get scrubbed up by you."
But the Son of God thought otherwise!
"No," said Jesus, "you baptize me.
So all who follow will agree,
That they should do as I have done
And get baptized—just everyone."

That put a brand-new light on things!
So John agreed and it was done.
And then God thundered—like a gun—
"This is my beloved son."

Two—He Changed It

Once long ago in a faraway time
Jesus went to a wedding that ran out of wine.
"Oh, Jesus," said Mary, "how much would you mind
To take jugs of water all in a line
Then order that water to turn into wine?"
But Jesus told Mary that he'd rather not
As he studied the water in six giant pots.
But he did love his mother and so to be kind
He told the wine server what God had in mind.
It was quite a surprise
When they filled up their glasses and toasted the bride.
They were stunned to observe that the water was wine.
This was the first miracle done at his hand.
For he'd just started out—brand-new in the land.
But he was so grand, they'd soon understand.
It's so much like Jesus to take something bland
And touch it with power and leave it more grand.

Three—He Walked on It

One foot up and one foot down,
Ocean strolling all around
Sandal slapping, Jesus found
He would walk where others drowned.
Once when all his friends were free
Jesus met them out at sea

Walking over Galilee.
Marching, marching—hut, two, three,
Walking out across the blue
Is something only God can do.

Four—He Ordered It Around

Once when the water was wicked
Once when a shout filled the clouds
Once when the seas were aroar
Once when the wind was too proud
Once when the thunder was booming
Once when the waves spoke out loud
Jesus got tired of the storm and the noise.
"All right—that's enough," he allowed.
"I can't sleep! Be still!" Then guess what?
The ocean behaved,
the wind stopped its yap.
So Jesus was pleased that he'd stilled the seas
And promptly lay down for a nap.

Five—He Claimed to Be It

I am the water of life without end.
Drink me and live forever, my friends.
One little gulp is what God intends,
Drink and you'll never be thirsty again.

Six—He Drank It

Once in Samaria perched on a well
Christ met a woman—they talked for a spell.
"You must be quite thirsty,

For I'm thirsty, too."
"Yes, give me a drink," said Jesus, "won't you?"
"Whoa, I can't just give out water to you,
Why, I'm a Samaritan, you are a Jew.
With Jews I have very little to do.
I'm ever so biased to men such as you."
What happened next? Well, what do you think?
Jesus convinced her as quick as a wink
To quit hating people—to drop that instinct—
And once she had done it, before you could blink,
She gave him the water, and he took a drink.

THE MAN WHO
SCRATCHED

William Griffin

Lepers were outcasts. People rejected them, leaving them not only diseased but very lonely. Jesus cured both the disease and their loneliness.

❧

Hello, I'm a leper." A man popped out from behind a building and stood right in front of Jesus. "Please don't run away."

"What's the matter with your skin?" asked Jesus.

"Can't you see? I'm covered with runny sores and crusty scabs. Nobody wants to look at me, my face is so horrible."

"What do you want me to do?"

"You can make me better. I know you can," said the man, falling on his knees in front of Jesus. "If you don't, I'll scratch myself to death."

Jesus felt sorry for the poor man.

"Don't touch me," said the man. "That's how you get it."

"I'm not afraid to touch you." Jesus reached down, took hold of the man's arms and pulled him to his feet.

The itching was gone. The sores started to dry. The scabs began to fall off.

"Thank you, thank you, thank you!" shouted the man. "What can I do to thank you?"

"You can go to the temple, show yourself to a priest, and say a prayer of thanks to God."

"Yes, yes, I will, I will," promised the man hurrying off.

"One more thing," said Jesus.

"Anything, anything," said the man.

"You don't have to tell what I just did."

"I won't tell a soul," agreed the man as he skipped toward Jerusalem.

But the man was so happy and the walk to the temple so long that he forgot. He told everyone he met.

And the lepers along the road began to look for the wonderful man with the healing touch.[1]

[1]William Griffin, "The Man Who Scratched" in *Jesus for Children* (Minneapolis: Winston Press, 1985), 39–40.

PETER, JAMES, AND JOHN

Traditional Child's Song

*Children love those songs that tell
the stories of Jesus.*

Peter, James and John, in a little sail boat,
Peter, James and John, in a little sail boat,
Peter, James and John, in a little sail boat,
Out on the deep blue sea.

Fished all night, caught no fishes,
Fished all night, caught no fishes,
Fished all night, caught no fishes,
Out on the deep blue sea.

Along came Jesus walking on the water,
Along came Jesus walking on the water,
Along came Jesus walking on the water,
Out on the deep blue sea.

Now the little sail boat's full of fishes,
Now the little sail boat's full of fishes,
Now the little sail boat's full of fishes,
Out on the deep blue sea.

THE UNSINKABLE ROCK

Calvin Miller

*In this account of one of Jesus' wonders, he invites
Peter to do a very scary thing—to walk on the water
with him. Peter had good intentions, but Jesus
helped him take a good honest look at himself.*

———————— ❧ ————————

Long, long ago,
When Peter was a little boy,
He used to watch the restless sea,
And throw in rocks to hear them fall,
So plunking and so splashingly.
The rocks he threw would gurgle down
And sink with chug-a-lugging sounds.

I'm quite a bit like Peter, too.
I like to throw in rocks, don't you?
Most every rock will sink, it's true.
But read this story if you think
That every rock will simply sink.

Back when Peter threw those rocks,
No one had names like me and you—
Names like Bob or Lora Lee
Or Bill or Phil or Tom or Sue!
Jesus' friends had longer names,
Like Matthew and Bartholomew.

Back then their names were long enough
To tell where they were from, it's true,
Like Lazarus of Bethany
By Olivet! Wow! Goodness! Whew!

Now Peter who was Jesus' friend
Grew up beside a silver sea.
No one called him Peter till
He was well past twenty-three.
And it wasn't Peter's mom or dad
From whom the name of Peter came.
No! Someone very special gave
Peter such a special name.

Can you guess who? One guess or two?
Two guesses, maybe even three?
If it wasn't Peter's mom,
Then whoever could it be?
His mother named him Simon of
Capernaum beside the sea.
That's quite a name!
Don't you agree?
(By the way that silver sea
Was called the Sea of Galilee.)

Well, Simon of Capernaum
Grew up. And then eventually
He bought himself a boat or two
And fished a lot on Galilee.

One day he dragged his boat ashore
To patch a soggy fishing net.
When suddenly he raised his eyes,
And wow, can you guess who he met?

Well! Can you guess? You're right! They met
And briskly hugged there in the sun—
"I'm Jesus Christ of Nazareth!"
"I'm Simon of Capernaum!"

Then Jesus spoke there by the dock.
"From now on, Simon, you're the Rock!
The Rock, I say, will be your name."
(Now Peter is the word for rock
In the language Jesus talked.)

Jesus then went on to say,
"You're a rock so very strong
I'm going to build My church upon
Your life and faith. And then you'll be
The Rock that holds My glorious church
Through time and all eternity."

"I'm Peter, but I'm still the same!
I simply have a brand new name.
This has been some day and how!
This morning I was Simon, wow!
Just look at me! I'm Peter now!"

Eleven other tall, strong men
Were also Jesus' special friends.
And all of them would sail the sea
Almost each day on Galilee.

It happened on a lovely day
When Jesus stayed behind to pray.
His twelve disciples sailed away,
But the sun did not stay warm.

The clouds rolled in and then a storm.

The thunder roared. The rain poured down.
The men cried, "Jesus help! We'll drown!"
But Jesus wasn't on the boat,
Which lurched and barely stayed afloat.

Jesus knelt upon the ground.
Still in His mind He heard the sound
Of friends all crying they would drown
Because the sea was upside down!

He knew He must go to His friends
But had no boat to get to them.
So He decided there and then
He'd walk across the sea to them.

Sound impossible to you?
It's not all that hard to do—
If you were just the Son of God.
Why, you could walk on any sea.
Just don't look down! Now that's the key!
Just right foot, left foot, one, two, three!

So Jesus walked out steppingly.
Right foot, left . . . Across the sea!
He saw His friends! And as they stared
Jesus saw those men were scared!

Know what scared His friends the most?
They thought that Jesus was a ghost.
I guess the lightning of the night
Made His robe look ghostly-bright
And gave His friends an awful fright.

When James and John Bar Zebedee
(Two of His friends from Galilee)

Saw Him standing on the sea,
They cried in fear, "What shall we do?"
"Hey, look at this, Bartholomew!"
Just then the fiery lightning flashed!
Bartholomew saw Jesus, too.
Another friend cried, "Help! Oh, whew!
Good grief, a ghost! What will we do?"

"Fear not . . . It's Me," was Jesus' plea,
"I'm walking to you on the sea."

"Oh, wow!" cried Peter, "If it's You,
I'd like to walk on water, too."

"Come on then, Peter; it's like the ground.
It's easy if you don't look down.
Just keep your eyes glued hard to Me,
You'll find it's easy as can be."

Peter jumped down on the sea.
He thought he'd sink in to his knees,
But boy, was he surprised and pleased.
And he just stood there as he grinned!
"Jesus, You are such a friend."

Peter then felt simply grand
That he could look at Christ and stand,
Or walk, or skip, as though he planned
A shopping trip on solid land!

Walking on the sea was fun!
And Peter knew it was God's Son
Who helped him get the walking done.
But Peter then became so proud
He very proudly said out loud,

"Gee! I can do this all alone."

He took his eyes off Christ . . . and well
He took one step and promptly fell.
The cold sea came up to his knees
And then his waist. He felt he'd freeze.
And as he tried to swim and grapple,
Water reached his Adam's apple.
And then it covered up his head.
He thought for sure he'd soon be dead.
"Help . . . Lord . . . Please help.
I've really flubbed.
Help, Jesus! Save me!
Glub! Glub! Glub!"

And Jesus reaching in the sea,
Pulled Peter back up on his feet,
And said, "Please, Rock, have faith in Me!
Why did you doubt? Believe, you'll see!"

The Rock then walked and stayed afloat
Till both of them got to the boat.
A friend who met them at the brink
Said "Peter, you're the rock! Just think
God made one Rock that couldn't sink."
And this just proves what you can do
If you have faith in Jesus, too.
You may never walk the sea,
But be the best kid you can be.
You can do things you would not think.
Ask the Rock that couldn't sink.[2]

---

[2]Calvin Miller, *The Unsinkable Rock* (Nashville: Thomas Nelson Publishing, 1987).

MARIONETTA

Calvin Miller

This selection is not a poem about Jesus, but it is about what he does in our lives.

Jesus once said, "Ye shall know the truth and the truth shall make you free." Marionetta illustrates that the only way we really can be free is to find spiritual freedom as a freedom of the heart. Only when we are free on the inside are we really free.

Marionetta wanted to be a real girl.
She was always on stage where she'd dance and she'd sing
But when everyone left the theater at night
Marionetta was stranded, still tied to her strings.
Her strings were five and they kept her alive,
One for each hand and one for each foot
And for the top of her head.
The other string dancers had warned her so often
That without her five strings she'd be dead,
But Marionetta would hang in the dark
When all of the children were gone,
She'd cry ever softly and wish for the light
And dream of a day without strings.
Then she'd be free to run down a walk
Or skate on a scooter through wide parking lots.

She'd run through a meadow and chase butterflies,
Climb trees without getting all tangled in knots,
She'd fly from her shadows and dance on the wind
And listen to locusts and katydids sing,
And she would be free as a robin or a swallow,
With never the tug or the yank of a string.

One night after acting she hung on a board
Her dark strings were knotted and twisted in cords.
"Marionetta," a kind voice spoke in the dark,
"Would you come with me to the mountains and sea
If I cut your strings so you could be free?"

"Yes, yes," she cried, "but I'm knotted in cords.
I'm hanging quite backwards and facing the boards."
"I'm the Master of Dancers, I'll cut all your strings
You'll dance in the light where the katydid sings."

The other string dancers began to object,
"Don't trust him, you'll die. He promises things
But our kind can't live or move without strings."
"I'd rather be dead than tied up in cords
All knotted in darkness and facing the boards,
Come, Master of Dancers, and cut off these strings."

In the dark Marionetta could not see a thing
As the string dancers' master drew near.
But she heard a brief snip and felt a string clipped
And her left leg fell free and dangled in air.

A second snip came and she hung splendidly
And two more short snips and her hands dangled free.
She hung by one string on the top of her head.
With one final snip she tumbled like lead
And the string dancers cried, "The poor girl is dead."

"Oh no, I'm not," said a voice in the dark,
"I'm free of the strings and I'll follow the lark."
When the morning light came on the edge of the dawn
Everyone saw Marionetta was gone.
They doubted the voice that had called in the night,
That promised the dancer a life in the light.
They hung in their cords, the poor knotted things,
Insisting that no one could live without strings.

But Marionetta knew sunshine and joy
And ran through the meadows where katydids sing.
She chased her fast shadow where waterfalls spring,
So glad she had chosen a life without strings.[3]

[3]Calvin Miller, "Marionetta" in *When the Aardvark Parked on the Ark* (Dallas: Word, 1984), 90.

"SERMON ON THE MOUNT"
CARL BLOCH

CHAPTER FOUR

FIVE THINGS JESUS TAUGHT US TO HELP MAKE THE WORLD A BETTER PLACE

HE TAUGHT THEM ALL THAT
THEY COULD UNDERSTAND.
MARK 4:33 (ICB)

Have you ever noticed how your grandpa spends all of his time watching the news or the weather channel? It's like he doesn't even know that there are movie channels or video games. It would probably be a good idea if you would sit down and watch the news with him sometime. This will probably amaze him. It may even please him. You don't have to sit there as long as he does, but watch it and you'll discover that there aren't many good things that get reported in the news. Usually there are stories of murders and wars and government swindles. It goes on and on, night after night, year after year. It's amazing that Grandpa stays as warm and cheerful as he does.

The world has always had a lot of bad stuff going on in it. People get killed or get some terrible disease or lose their freedom, or they are forced to leave their homes because of invasions. Jesus himself lived in a time when the Romans were in charge of the world. They made his homeland a horrible place to live. They wouldn't let Jesus or any of his fellow Jews be citizens. They believed that Jews were inferior to Romans. People who are in charge often believe that those they control are inferior to them. The Romans never let the Jews vote on anything. They sold the Jews as slaves and forced them to do hard work for no money. People back then suffered because of evil rulers and tricky politicians just like they do today.

But Jesus thought it shouldn't be that way. Jesus thought the world should have better newscasts. And so he taught us five things—five things that, if they were put into effect, would indeed make the world a wonderful place to live. What were those five things?

First, Jesus taught the Golden Rule. The Golden Rule is this: Do unto others as you would have them do unto you. We should never do anything to anyone that we would not want them to do to us. If only people would practice this rule, all crime and war would cease. Imagine what would happen if every thief who was about to steal something from someone asked, "Would I want this person to steal something from me?" What if every murderer, as he pointed a gun at someone and started to pull the trigger, would ask, "Would I want someone to do this to me?" I think you can see how the Golden Rule would change the world instantly if people just started to do it. The same is true for the other four things that Jesus taught us we would have to do to make the world a better place to live.

Second, Jesus taught us the Great Commandment. The Great Commandment is to love God with all our hearts and our neighbors as ourselves. Some neighbors can be pretty mean and pretty hard to love. But you yourself are somebody's neighbor. Are you ever mean? Are you ever hard to live with? Wouldn't you rather your neighbor loved you anyway? Funny, but that's how your neighbor feels, too.

Third, Jesus taught us that we should pray. He even taught us how to pray. But how would that make our world better? Well, have you ever noticed that it's impossible to swindle or steal or murder while you're praying? Think of this: There has never been one bank robbery committed by people who are known to pray a lot. Jesus knew that, too. In fact, have you ever tried to get God to listen to you while you criticized others in your prayer? God never listens to gossip or slander in prayers. No, when we talk to God, we just don't get critical about others. Why? Because we know that God doesn't like listening to us gossip about those people we criticize.

Fourth, Jesus taught us not to be uppity. Do you like uppity people? You should like them, but uppity is one thing that is very hard to admire. Uppity people often feel superior to people who they think are not as wonderful as they are. The Pharisees felt that Jesus was far too easy on people who sinned more than they did. Jesus reminded them that while the Pharisees didn't commit sins that they could get caught at, they were very guilty of the sin of uppityness. Jesus said that we should all try to be humble and not be proud of it.

Fifth, Jesus taught us the Great Commission. We call this the Great Commission because what Jesus asked us to do in the Great Commission was his whole reason for coming to earth in the first place. This Great Commission contained the last words Jesus ever said in this world before he went back to heaven. Usually, the last words that anybody says are the words that they consider the most important or they would have said them earlier in life when they were talking about trivial things. Jesus wanted everybody to know about God's love. The only way we can teach people that God loves them is to be loving as we teach them.

These five teachings are the most important things that Jesus taught about how to make the world a better place to live. Everybody can see how they would change the world for the better if they were really carried out. But not many people actually put them into practice. Maybe we should go ahead and try to do all of these things Jesus taught, even if the rest of the world seems unlikely to do them. Then at least we would be doing all we can to make the world a better place to live.

Till then, I suppose, Grandpa will continue to watch the news channel. He is going to see a lot of bad stuff happening all around the world. But have you ever noticed that Grandpa smiles a lot? Do you suppose that he knows that most of the world is doing it wrong, and he knows there's a better way? Grandpas often know more about these five things Jesus taught than we think they do.

THE GREAT COMMANDMENT: LOVE ONE ANOTHER

Matthew 22:36–40 (TLB)

Moses said there were ten commandments. Jesus believed that we should honor all ten commandments, but that the great commandment was that we should love one another.

∝

Sir, which is the most important command in the laws of Moses?"

Jesus replied, " 'Love the Lord your God with all your heart, soul, and mind.' This is the first and greatest commandment. The second most important is similar: 'Love your neighbor as much as you love yourself.' All the other commandments and all the demands of the prophets stem from these two laws and are fulfilled if you obey them. Keep only these and you will find that you are obeying all the others."

" U ":
THE GREAT
COMMISSION

Calvin Miller

The Great Commission was this: "Go into all the world and tell the good news to everyone who will listen." These are the last words that Jesus ever said. What is the good news? Just this: Everyone is loved by God. Those who suffer from loneliness and despair have great hope.

One time, before time, a long time ago
Before there were dewdrops and raindrops or snow,
Before there were people and places you'd know
And way before hot dogs or burgers to go.

God looked and saw there was nothing to see,
And so he said plainly, "Things are too bleak.
I'm going to make 'stuff' for one solid week—
Like stars, worlds and mountains, and rivers and creeks—
So let there be stuff, even now as I speak."

He worked for five days, and then took a peek!
"Wow! Look what I've done with my creative week!
But now it's day six, I'll do something unique."

Make local inhabitant folks (so to speak),
Like Mandarins, Muscovites, Hebrews and Greeks
And Asians and Aussies and folks Mozambique."

So God filled his world with people like you.
In fact there are now 6 billion and two.
Does this seem too many? Does this seem too few?
Does it seem that with this many people in view,
That God might not care about little old you?

Does God really care for and love you? You bet!
God's love is as real as love ever gets!

Like the 21st letter of your alphabet
It's a wonderful letter, I'm sure you have met.
It's the letter called U. U know it I'm sure.
For without this small letter, U couldn't endUre.

The day U were born, U became very U.
U-niquer than U ever thought U could do.
You're Ultra-utopian, Ultra true blue,
Utterly Ultimate, Utterly U.

Don't U suppose
God knows that it's true
That you're U-er than anyone else
That U knew.
You're U-er
Than me,
Or Tommy
Or Drew
You're U-er
Than Billy

Or Bobby
Or Sue.

So see, you're important! Say, how do U do!
You're just pretty special, you wonderful U!
Before U were thought of or time had begun,
God even stuck U in the name of his son.
And each time U pray—you'll see it is true—
You can't spell out JesUs and not include U.

You're a pretty big part of his wonderful name.
For U he was born—that's why he came.
And his great love for U is the reason he died.
It even takes U to spell crUcified.

Isn't it thrilling and splendidly grand.
He rose from the dead, with U in his plan.
The stones split away, the gold trUmpet blew,
And this word resUrrection is spelled with a U.

When Jesus left earth at his upward ascension,
He felt there was one thing he just had to mention.
"Go into the world and tell them it's true
That I love them all just like I love U."

Who are all these U's who are so much like U?
Who just want to know that God loves them too?
Why they're Utes and Ubangis and Upper Voltarians.
Some are Uppity folks from Upstate in Barrelton.
They're folks from Upsala or old Uruguay
From Utah or Yuma or Upper Calais
Or Urrey or Ulster or lower Ukraine
Or Upper Uganda or Uppermost Spain.

Think of Manchuria and all the ManchUs,
Or lower Banturia with all the BantUs
Or PerU or HonshU or North MalibU.

So many great people are spelled with a U,
Somewhere around three hundred and two.
Do you love them all like Jesus loves U?
He'd like for them all to have friends it is true
But Jesus is waiting on what U will do.
Yes, you are the key—it all starts with U.[1]

[1]Calvin Miller, " 'U': What Jesus Wants Us To Do," (Richmond, Va.: Foreign Missions Magazine, 1996), insert.

THE GIRL WHO DIED

William Griffin

Jesus could heal people of their diseases. He could even heal the dead with life.

❧

My girl, my daughter, she's only twelve years old, and she's dying!"

Jesus was standing by the lakeside with friends when the man ran up to him. His name was Jairus; he was one of the officials of the synagogue.

"Please come and save her. Touch her, and she will get better."

Jesus went with the man.

Halfway to Jairus's house people ran up to them with the bad news. "You're too late! Your daughter is dead! No one can help her now!"

Jairus looked at Jesus. "Don't worry," said Jesus. "It's not too late. Trust me."

When the two of them arrived at the house the relatives and neighbors were already crying because the girl was dead.

"Why all the sad noise?" asked Jesus. "The child is not dead. She's only asleep."

Jesus then went into the room where the child lay, approached the bed, and took her hand.

He prayed for a while and then said to her, "Wake up, child."

She began to breathe again.

"It's time to get up."

She got up from the bed and walked slowly around the room.

Her mother and father were astonished.

"She must be hungry," Jesus said to her parents. "Give her something to eat."

As he was leaving, Jesus asked the family not to tell what happened to anyone else. But word got around.[2]

---

[2]Griffin, "The Girl Who Died," 53–54.

THE GOLDEN RULE: NEEDLES

Calvin Miller

This story in rhyme illustrates the truth of the Golden Rule: Do unto others as you would have them do unto you.

───── ❊ ─────

Needles Potts
Loved to give shots,
With a long square needle
And a two-quart syringe.
Above the knee-joint
He would jab in the point
And laughing in vigor
He'd squeeze on the trigger
While the children he treated
Would whimper and cringe.

He'd often give babies
Shots to cure rabies
Though babies with rabies
Are really quite rare.
He'd simply say
Maybe this baby has rabies
I'd better just wheedle
My needle in here.

Yes most of his pleasure
Came from the children.
He'd stick in his needle
And laugh through the day.
He'd stick it in fast and
Twist it and laugh.
Some places he'd put it
We really can't say.
He'd stick it in knees
And elbows and thighs
While kiddies all cried.

One day it happened,
Needles Potts became ill.
He went to a doctor
Who studied him well
And said very gravely
"My dear Needles Potts,
You have a condition

That cannot be cured.
My poor Dr. Potts
This sad word I give,
You must have every day
Some thirty-two shots,
Yes, thirty-two shots
For as long as you live.
Your case, Dr. Potts,
Is most horrid, I fear,
Thirty-two daily,
Have I made myself clear?
That's eleven thousand
And more shots a year."

He started to cry.
His doctor said, "Needles,
You're crying, but why?
I thought you liked shots."
"I hate shots," said Potts.
"Shots are not fun
If I get the stabbing,
They only bring joy
When I do the jabbing."

There ever after
The good Dr. Potts
Got thousands and thousands
And thousands of shots.

So if you like causing anyone pain
Remember his story again and
again.
Be gentle and kind and ever alert
Never to laugh when anyone
hurts,
And then ask yourself,
"Just what would you do
If the hurt of another
Was given to you."
Remember the fate
Of poor Needles Potts
Who as far as I know
Still suffers lots
Getting thousands and thousands
And thousands of shots.[3]

---

[3]Calvin Miller, "Needles" in *When the Aardvark Parked on the Ark* (Dallas: Word, 1984), 122.

THE LORD'S PRAYER

Matthew 6:9–13 (KJV)

*Jesus taught us to pray using this—the most famous
of all prayers—as our model prayer.*

Our Father which art in heaven,
Hallowed be thy name.
Thy kingdom come.
Thy will be done in earth, as it is in heaven.
Give us this day our daily bread.
And forgive us our debts,
as we forgive our debtors.
And lead us not into temptation,
but deliver us from evil:
For thine is the kingdom, and the power, and the glory,
for ever. Amen.

NOT TO BE UPPITY: THE WASHING OF FEET
John 13:3–17 (TLB)

Jesus took a basin and towel to do something his disciples felt was beneath them. Jesus says all kinds of service are useable to God, and nothing that Jesus was willing to do should be rejected by us.

✧

Jesus knew that the Father had given him everything and that he had come from God and would return to God. And how he loved his disciples! So he got up from the supper table, took off his robe, wrapped a towel around his loins, poured water into a basin, and began to wash the disciples' feet and to wipe them with the towel he had around him.

When he came to Simon Peter, Peter said to him, "Master, you shouldn't be washing our feet like this!"

Jesus replied, "You don't understand now why I am doing it; some day you will."

"No," Peter protested, "you shall never wash my feet!"

"But if I don't, you can't be my partner," Jesus replied.

Simon Peter exclaimed, "Then wash my hands and head as well—not just my feet!"

Jesus replied, "One who has bathed all over needs only to have his feet washed to be entirely clean. Now you are clean—but that isn't true of everyone here." For Jesus knew who would betray him. That is what he meant when he said, "Not all of you are clean."

After washing their feet he put on his robe again and sat down and asked, "Do you understand what I was doing? You call me 'Master' and 'Lord,' and you do well to say it, for it is true. And since I, the Lord and Teacher, have washed your feet, you ought to wash each other's feet. I have given you an example to follow: do as I have done to you. How true it is that a servant is not greater than his master. Nor is the messenger more important than the one who sends him. You know these things—now do them!"

"LIGHT OF THE WORLD"
CORBERT GAUTHIER

FIVE OF
THE BEST
SHORT
STORIES
JESUS
EVER TOLD

THEN HE TOLD THEM MANY THINGS
IN PARABLES.
MATTHEW 13:3 (NIV)

Jesus is the world's best-known storyteller. He told more than eighteen major stories as parts of his sermons. Sometimes, when people would ask him a question, he would put his answer to the question in terms of a story. For instance, when someone asked him, "Who is my neighbor?" he told one of his most impressive stories, the story of the Good Samaritan. This story is particularly significant because in it Jesus defines a neighbor as someone of a different racial background. So he not only answered the question but did it in a way that would help people see that hating anyone of a different racial background would hurt the heart of their heavenly Father.

Once Peter became concerned as to just how often he ought to forgive someone who kept on doing him wrong over and over. Peter felt that after he had forgiven someone seven times for mistreating him it would be enough. But just to be sure that he was being fair about it, he asked Jesus, "Lord, how many times shall I forgive a person who keeps on doing me wrong? Is seven times enough?" Once again on this occasion Jesus answered Peter by telling him a story. The story was about a merciless man who owed over ten thousand talents of silver to his debtor. It was a huge debt. The deadline came near, and the man who was in debt knew he could not pay any of the money back. But he begged his creditor, "Please, sir, be patient with me and I will pay it all back in a little while." There is little need to tell the story here since it is one of the five great stories that Jesus told and is included in this section.

Many times Jesus told stories to help make difficult ideas easier. People in every generation are always asking, "Why are there so many hypocrites in the church?" Jesus knew that in any good organization there are likely to be some bad people, making all the good people look bad. So Jesus told the story of a man who planted a whole field of wheat, and then an enemy came along and sowed weed seeds in with the grains of wheat. There they were, lots of weeds growing up with the grain. Jesus said it would be better not to try to pull out the weeds lest some of the good wheat be uprooted in the process. The best time to deal with the weeds was after the grain had been ripe and harvested. Then the weeds could be destroyed and the grain would not be hurt.

Once, to demonstrate how much God loved ordinary people, Jesus told three stories of people who lost something very precious to them. He told first of a shepherd who lost one of his one hundred sheep. This shepherd left the ninety-nine that were safe and went out in search of the poor lost lamb. He looked all over for it until he finally found it. Then when he found it, he called in his neighbors and they threw a big party celebrating the finding of the lost sheep. After that he told of a woman who had ten coins and lost one of them. She was frantic, looking everywhere until she found it. Then she also called her neighbors and they threw a party, celebrating the finding of the lost coin. The third story that Jesus told was of a man who had two sons and lost one of them. When the lost boy came home, the father threw a party and called in all his neighbors and they celebrated long and joyously over the finding of this lost boy. The point of all three of these stories is that when people who are lost to all human meaning and real purpose are found, then God himself rejoices and so do the angels in heaven.

Jesus also told stories to give his disciples an inside track on some difficult truths about the Kingdom of God that nobody else needed to know about. On one occasion he said to them, "The secrets of the Kingdom of God have been given to you so that those who are not Christians will not be tempted to try to understand things too difficult for them." After saying this he told them the parable of the soils. This parable made perfect sense to his disciples but would not be so easily interpreted or misused by those outside his close circle of friends.

Most of Jesus' stories were used to illustrate very practical things, like why and how God answers our prayers. Jesus told a story of a persistent, poor woman who needed a judge to help her with a lawsuit against a man who was trying to keep her in poverty. The judge really didn't like the poor woman and was prone to disregard her many pleas, but she was so constantly troublesome that the judge finally gave in. "Even though I don't fear God or care about men, yet because this widow keeps bothering me, I will see that she gets justice, so that she won't eventually wear me out with her coming." Jesus used this little story to talk about how important it was for us to keep on praying to God for those things that only God can give us.

So the stories of Christ were very central to all of his teaching. But between you and me, I think Jesus also used a lot of stories because he knew that stories make sermons more interesting. Have you ever tried to listen to a preacher who never told any stories? I wonder if Jesus once had a storyless rabbi. I wonder if as a boy he had listened to a lot of sermons in the synagogue that were boring beyond belief. Maybe it was back then that he made up his mind he would become a great storyteller.

THE JAUNTY GENTILE

Calvin Miller

*Prejudice is a way of making our enemies less
human than they are by making them so much less
than we feel we are. Jesus confronted prejudice
in a very effective way. He celebrated a
Samaritan, whom his own race of people were
prone to condemn.*

*This story is a tale Jesus told to illustrate how
important it is to be kind. The story is found in
Luke 10:25–37. Jesus told the story in a better way
than I am telling it, but sometimes you remember a
story better when it is told in a little different way.
Dear children, remember how important it is to
celebrate stories just as Jesus told them. Still, I
don't think Jesus would mind us telling
the story in this way.*

Once a lawyer asked Jesus, "Who is my neighbor?"
Jesus told the following tale—

Once in Judea there was a Jewish gent
    Who journeyed out of Jerusalem jogging toward Jericho.
But he hadn't journeyed very far when some giant
    Gypsies jumped him, high-jacking his journey
    By jabbing him in the jaw and the jugular.

With blows to the head, they left him half-dead,
Bloody and red and seven furlongs from a hospital bed.

So . . .
This poor jilted Jew was but a gelatinous
    Jar of ginger jelly
And was almost to die when along came a Priest
    Who saw him writhing and moaning and
    Holding his belly.
"Jeepers," he jabbered. "Jehovah is just, so jump up and I'll join you on your
    Journey to Jericho."
"I can't jump up . . . I'm juiced," jibed the Jewish gent. "I've been
    Jabbed in the jaw and the jugular by some
    Junkies who jumped me."

"Please can you help me get by?
If not I'm a goner and likely to die."

"Sorry," said the priest. "But let me give you some advice:
    Trust God and stop bleeding;
    Bleeding is a leading cause of death."
    Then he went on his way.

Then came along a Levite,
"Jumpin' Jehoshaphat! Who jabbed you in the jaw
    And the jugular?" jibed the Levite.
"Some giant gypsies. I've been seriously jarred.
    You're Jewish, I'm Jewish, can you help me?
If not I'm juiced," gestured the poor Jewish gent.

"Surely you jest! I'm freshly pressed
    And neatly dressed.
But let me give you some advice: Trust God and stop bleeding;
Bleeding is a leading cause of death."

The Levite left and along came a jaunty

Gentile leading a donkey.

"Jumpin' Geronimo! Who jumped you?"

"Some giant gypsies who jabbed me in the

Jaw and the jugular.

Can you help me?"

"Well I guess so even though you're a

Jewish gent and I'm only a jaunty Gentile.

But first I'd better just bandage your wounds and splint your bones.

I'll stop your bleeding and you stop your groans."

In an hour the jaunty Gentile had taken

The Jewish gent to a small hotel in Jericho,

Emptied his purse, hired a nurse,

Making everything better than it once was.

"Well," said Jesus, "who do you think was neighbor to the man who fell among thieves?"

Everybody voted for the jaunty Gentile.

THE WISE MAN BUILT HIS HOUSE

Child's Song

*To build a secure life, the foundation must be
unshakeable, taught Jesus. The wise man was wise
because he understood the importance of a strong
foundation. The foolish man was foolish because he
paid no attention to the issue of foundations. The
wise man realized that a great life can withstand
any storm that comes its way
because it is well founded.*

The wise man built his house upon the rock,
The wise man built his house upon the rock,
The wise man built his house upon the rock,
And the rain came tumbling down.

The rain came down and the floods came up,
The rain came down and the floods came up,
The rain came down and the floods came up,
And the house on the rock stood firm.

The foolish man built his house upon the sand,
The foolish man built his house upon the sand,
The foolish man built his house upon the sand,
And the rain came tumbling down.

The rain came down and the floods came up,
The rain came down and the floods came up,
The rain came down and the floods came up,
And the house on the sand went smash.

So build your house on the Lord Jesus Christ,
So build your house on the Lord Jesus Christ,
So build your house on the Lord Jesus Christ,
And the blessings will come down.

The blessings come down as the prayers go up,
The blessings come down as the prayers go up,
The blessings come down as the prayers go up,
So build your house on the Lord Jesus Christ.

THE SINNER WHO WAS SORRY

William Griffin

The parables of Christ are "world stories" known and loved around the globe. This perhaps stands at the top of them all. This tale is the story of God's love for people who can say "I'm sorry" to people they've hurt. Once again, William Griffin's retelling of this tale for children sets Jesus' stories in a children's world so the world of their parents may be a better one.

~

What happens when a sinner is sorry for his or her sins?" people often asked Jesus.

"Let me answer your question," Jesus would say, "by telling you a story."

A young man was walking the long road home. His father ran to meet him.

"Where have you been?" asked the father.

"A long, long way from home," said the young man.

"Where's the money I gave you?"

"I spent it."

"What have you got to show for it?"

"Nothing."

"No clothes?"

"Just the rags I've got on."

"You look thin."

"I haven't eaten for days."

"How come you're so dirty?"

"My last job was taking care of pigs."

"You look it," said the father.

"Father, I've been thinking."

"That's a good start."

"I've sinned against God. I've sinned against you. I'm sorry," said the young man. "Well, aren't you going to slug me?"

"No."

"Why not?"

"I'm going to give you a party," said the father.

"But I don't deserve it."

"And I'm inviting everybody to come."

The father threw his arms around the young man's neck. The young man kissed his father. And they headed down the road toward home.

"But I don't want to go to his party," said the father's other son.

"Why not?" asked the father.

"It's not fair. You never gave me a party."

"Why should I?"

"I didn't run away from home," said the other son. "I stayed home and worked."

"May I tell you something?" the father asked his son. "Just between you and me?"

"What?"

"When your brother left home, your mother and I never heard from him. We thought he was dead. Seeing him again is like having him brought back from the dead."

"I never thought of it like that," said the other son.

"When you and I are together," said the father, "it's always good times. Let's go into the party," said the father, putting his arm around his son's shoulder, "and get something to eat. A little singing. A little dancing. It will be our party too."[1]

---

[1]Griffin, "The Sinner Who Was Sorry," 69.

THE FIVE FOOLISH VIRGINS

Matthew 25:1–13 (THE MESSAGE)

The foolish bridesmaids were unprepared for a long wait. Jesus used the story to remind everyone who heard it that all who love him should stay prepared for his second coming.

☙

God's kingdom is like ten young virgins who took oil lamps and went out to greet the bridegroom. Five were silly and five were smart. The silly virgins took lamps, but no extra oil. The smart virgins took jars of oil to feed their lamps. The bridegroom didn't show up when they expected him, and they all fell asleep.

In the middle of the night someone yelled out, "He's here! The bridegroom's here! Go out and greet him!"

The ten virgins got up and got their lamps ready. The silly virgins said to the smart ones, "Our lamps are going out; lend us some of your oil."

They answered, "There might not be enough to go around; go buy your own."

They did, but while they were out buying oil, the bridegroom arrived. When everyone who was there to greet him had gone into the wedding feast, the door was locked.

Much later, the other virgins, the silly ones, showed up and knocked on the door, saying, "Master, we're here. Let us in."

He answered, "Do I know you? I don't think I know you."

So stay alert. You have no idea when he might arrive.[2]

---

[2]Eugene Peterson, "The Five Foolish Virgins," Matthew 25:1–13 in *The Message* (Colorado Springs: Navpress, 1993), 63.

THE UNMERCIFUL SERVANT

Matthew 18:23–35 (CEV)

The unmerciful servant was unwilling to give others the forgiveness he wanted for himself. This story demonstrates what Jesus taught us about prayer in the Lord's Prayer: We are to forgive others their trespasses, as God forgives ours.

This story will show you what the kingdom of heaven is like:

One day a king decided to call in his officials and ask them to give an account of what they owed him. As he was doing this, one official was brought in who owed him fifty million silver coins. But he didn't have any money to pay what he owed. The king ordered him to be sold, along with his wife and children and all he owned, in order to pay the debt.

The official got down on his knees and began begging, "Have pity on me, and I will pay you every cent I owe!"

The king felt sorry for him and let him go free. He even told the official that he did not have to pay back the money.

As the official was leaving, he happened to meet another official, who owed him a hundred silver coins. So he grabbed the man by the throat. He started choking him and said, "Pay me what you owe!"

The man got down on his knees and began begging, "Have pity on me, and I will pay you back."

But the first official refused to have pity. Instead, he went and had the other official put in jail until he could pay what he owed.

When some other officials found out what had happened, they felt sorry for the man who had been put in jail. Then they told the king what had happened. The king called the first official back in and said, "You're an evil man! When you begged for mercy, I said you did not have to pay back a cent. Don't you think you should show pity to someone else, as I did to you?" The king was so angry that he ordered the official to be tortured until he could pay back everything he owed.

That is how my Father in heaven will treat you if you don't forgive each of my followers with all your heart.

"NEW DAY"
RICHARD STERGULZ

CHAPTER SIX

WHEN

JESUS

DIED

THE SOLDIERS TWISTED TOGETHER A CROWN
OF THORNS AND PUT IT ON HIS HEAD.
JOHN 19:2A (NIV)

What was the real reason that Jesus died? Did he die because the Romans had caught him and crucified him? Did he die because he couldn't get away from the authorities? That's certainly how it looked. But Jesus said he was the Son of God and that he had all power. This must certainly have included the power to get away from the police and escape from the soldiers. He even said that if he wished, God would send legions of angels to beat the daylights out of those soldiers who were about to execute him. He said that no one was taking his life from him but that he was freely dying of his own volition; his death would not be the result of someone taking his life from him against his will.

When people write books and they ask any question like the one at the top of this page, you get the sneaking suspicion that they really know and they're just making you guess wrong until they tell you the right answer. Well, here is the right answer: Jesus died because he wanted to live in this world, doing everything that people who live in this world have to do. One of the things we all have to do is die. So Jesus died.

People die in all kinds of ways. Sometimes they die of old age. It can happen after a person reaches the age of seventy or eighty years. Some important part of their bodies just quits working and they die. Some die when they are young. Some die in horrible accidents, some die in their sleep. But one thing characterizes most who die: They would just rather not do it. Often they have to go through a lot of pain. Or maybe they are afraid of death. The truth is that it is just more fun, generally speaking, to be alive than to be dead. But like it or not, everybody has to do it.

If Jesus was going to really be like us and help us understand how to deal with everything we have to face in life, he was going to have to show us how to die. So he did. It was in the spring of A.D. 27 when he died. He was put to death in a very horrible way. He was nailed to a cross. There he was hanging by his hands, and the pain was excruciating. He cried out seven times as he hung there. You can count them all up if you read the story of his death in the Bible. The seven last sentences that Jesus cried out were these:

First: "Take care of my mother," he said to his friend John. And then, turning to his mother, he said, "Mother, John is my friend. Help him deal with his grief." These two statements are considered his first cross cry.

Second: "Father, forgive them!" he said to God, in prayer, asking God to forgive those who were taking his life.

THE BOOK OF JESUS FOR FAMILIES

Third: "Today you will be with me in Paradise," he said to another person—an executed criminal who was dying beside him.

Fourth: "I thirst!" he said, because all of his suffering had made his mouth so dry.

Fifth: "My God, my God! Why have you forsaken me?" he asked his Father in heaven, for his pain was so great it seemed like God must not care about him.

Sixth: "It is finished!" he said just before he died. Notice that he did not say "I am finished!" but "It is finished!" indicating that it was not his life that was through—he would indeed live again—but the plan of God for all the ages had been finished.

Seventh: "Father, into thy hands I commend my spirit," he said. Then he coughed a little blood, and his life was gone.

After saying all these things, he died. They took his body down from the cross. Then they ran a spear in his side—just in case he looked dead but really wasn't, the spear would make sure he was.

Since we all have to die, maybe we should ask ourselves, what did Jesus teach us about dying that will make it easier for us to do it when the time comes? He taught us three things. First, even if we should have to die in some very painful way like Jesus did, even while we're dying we can talk to God like Jesus did. Of his seven cross cries, four of them were made directly to God. This indicates that God was listening to him and cared about him as he died. This will be true of us as well. We won't have to die alone. We will have God's listening presence all the way through the death experience.

Second, even when we are dying, we should not allow the pain of it to keep us from thinking of other people. Jesus does not cry out, "Please, somebody, come and feel sorry for me. Can't you see I'm dying?" No, count them in the list above. Three of his cross cries were in the interest of other people, and three more of the seven were brief conversations he was having with his Father. Only one of them—namely "I thirst"— was in his own self-interest, and he only cried out that one because his mouth was so dry that he couldn't talk to anybody.

Third, death is not permanent. The moment that we close our eyes in death in this life, we are still going to be alive somewhere. Jesus certainly did not pass out of existence when he died. He just changed addresses. He did have an earthly location, but the moment that he closed his eyes in death, he opened them in heaven. On earth, to those who watched him die, it still looked like he was dead. But Jesus proved three days later when he walked out of the tomb that however things look on earth, we are always alive somewhere.

Jesus' death was so much in the interest of other people that it cannot be denied that he truly died for others. He gave his own life so that all could know how much he loved them. He loved us all so much that he gave all he could give. A little child once asked his father, "Just how big was Jesus' love?" The father said, "My child, Jesus loved you this much." The father stretched out his hands to show his child how Jesus died on the cross.

Now do you see why the church is so fascinated with crosses? Do you see why we put crosses on our steeples and over our altars and wear them on chains around our necks? We love crosses because they remind us that Jesus loved us so much that he died on a cross for us. It's hard not to love a man like Jesus.

THE CRUCIFIXION

Pearl S. Buck

Consider the events that describe the day Jesus died.

⊕

It was still early on that long morning of trial and condemnation when Jesus started his last and most painful journey.

The Roman soldiers led him through the north gate of the city to the place of death, called Calvary by the Romans and known as Golgotha in the Hebrew tongue. Both names mean "The Place of the Skull." Jesus staggered up the hillside carrying the heavy cross upon which he was later to be nailed, for it was the custom among the Romans that those who were about to die by execution should carry their own crosses.

His back was bowed beneath the weight of the great wooden beam as he walked, and his feet stumbled on the rough road. A great company of people gathered and followed him as he slowly climbed the hill to Calvary. Some were enemies who mocked him, some were passing strangers who joined the throng through curiosity or chance, and some were his friends who longed to help him but could not. The women among them wailed and wept, lamenting Jesus and beating their breasts with sorrow as they saw his suffering and knew that worse was yet to come.

And even with the racking pain in his body and the cross upon his back, Jesus saw their sorrow. He turned his head to them and said: "Daughters of Jerusalem, do not weep for me. Weep rather for yourselves and for your children, for a time is coming when it will be said, 'Happy are the childless, who have no little ones to be slain, and happy are those who never will have children.' For when Jerusalem suffers for its sins it will be well for those who have no young ones, for not even the youngest will be spared. And at that time the people of the city will say to the mountains, 'Fall on us!' and to the hills they will cry, 'Cover us!' so that they might escape their fate. But there will be no escape, for if this is what they do when I am here, what will they do when I am gone?"

He stumbled on beneath the cross, carrying it upon his wounded shoulders. But he had been so badly beaten that his strength was almost gone, and at last he fell and could not rise. The soldiers cursed and prodded him. But still he could not manage to struggle to his feet with the weight upon his back.

"You, there!" the soldiers shouted, and they seized upon a man in the crowd who knew nothing of what was happening. The man was Simon of Cyrene, who was coming in from the country; and they laid the cross upon his back and compelled him to carry it after Jesus. Jesus therefore rose and walked on slowly.

The procession continued. Now two other doomed men, common criminals, were brought into it to be led with Jesus to the place of death.

At last they all reached the Place of the Skull. When they came to the hilltop the soldiers ordered Simon of Cyrene to lay the cross down flat upon the ground. Then they removed Jesus' clothes and made him lie upon the cross. They nailed him to it through his hands and feet. Now they raised the cross and planted it firmly in the earth. Meanwhile, other guards were preparing the two criminals for crucifixion, and when the three crosses were raised Jesus was in the center with one robber on his right hand and the other on his left.

The soldiers offered Jesus a drink of sour wine mixed with bitter gall, but he refused it. And as he hung there on the cross awaiting death, Jesus called out: "Father, forgive them, for they know not what they do."

There was little to do but wait. While they waited, the soldiers divided up the clothes that Jesus had been wearing into four parts, one for each man guarding him while he slowly died. But when they came to the tunic and saw that, instead of having a seam, it was woven in one piece from top to bottom, they decided that it could not be divided. Therefore they said to one another, "Let us not tear it, but cast lots among us to see who shall have it." They did so, and in doing it they fulfilled the psalm in the scriptures which read: "They divided my garments among them, and for my clothing they cast lots." All these things the Roman soldiers did, without knowing that what they were doing had been predicted centuries before.

Now Pilate had written a sign in letters of Hebrew, Latin, and Greek, saying: "THIS IS JESUS THE KING OF THE JEWS." When the soldiers had finished their business of dividing up the clothes they set the sign over Jesus' head and settled back to watch him die.

The people stood there staring at him. Others, passing by along the road, stopped to jeer at him and shake their heads in scorn.

"You who would destroy the temple and build it up again in three days, save yourself!" they mocked. "If you are the Son of God, save yourself and come down from the cross." The chief priests, with the scribes and elders, mocked him in the same way, saying: "He saved others, so we hear, but he cannot save himself. He is the Christ, the King of Israel and the chosen one of God! Therefore let him now come down from the cross, and we will believe in him. He trusted in God; let God now deliver him if he wants to. For this man said, 'I am the Son of God.' "

But though Jesus could have come down from the cross he would not, for death on the cross was his destiny.

The soldiers mocked him, too. They came to him offering him sour wine to moisten his dry lips, and said: "If you are the King of the Jews, let us see you save yourself!"

Even the robbers who were being crucified alongside him abused him. One in particular mocked and cursed at Jesus. "Are you not the Christ?" he said. "If you are, save yourself and us!"

But as the time passed and the first man received no answer, the second man began to see in Jesus a quiet strength he had not seen before. He therefore rebuked the other, saying, "Have you no fear even of God, when you are suffering the same penalty as this man? We two are suffering justly, for we deserve to die for what we have done, but this man has done nothing wrong." Then he turned his head to look at Jesus. "Lord," he said, "remember me when you come into your kingdom, for I believe in you."

And Jesus answered him, saying, "I tell you truly, today you will be with me in Paradise."

Then he looked down to see those who stood near him. Close to the cross, stood his mother, his mother's sister, and Mary Magdalene, and only one of his disciples. Both Lazarus, whom he had raised from the dead, and the eleven men who had been his most devoted followers, were still in danger from the vengeful priests and Pharisees. Most of them, therefore, were afraid to be seen near him even while he was dying on the cross. But John at least, whom Jesus dearly loved, was there with the wailing women.

When Jesus saw John standing at his mother Mary's side and trying to comfort her, he called down from the cross. To his mother he said: "Woman, behold your son John!" And to John he said: "John, behold your mother! Care for her." And from that hour

John took Mary into his own home and cared for her as if she were his mother.

The painful hours dragged by. High noon came, and the sun blazed overhead. Then suddenly the sun was covered by black clouds and darkness fell over all the land. A strong wind swept the hill upon which the crosses stood, an eerie sound in the strange darkness of the day. Many of the people shook with fear and many of them left the place of death, trying to escape their fear. But many others, friends and enemies alike, stayed to see the end.

Three hours later, under a sky still ominously dark, Jesus cried out suddenly: "My God, my God, why have you forsaken me?" His hearers recognized the words, for they were also in the scriptures that had foretold the manner of his death. There was a brief silence, and the sky began to brighten.

Then Jesus spoke again, once more fulfilling the scriptures. "I thirst," he said.

There was a bowl of the sour wine standing by. One of the watchers took a sponge and soaked it in the wine, then put it on a reed and held it up so that Jesus might drink. And some of the others jeered, saying: "Let us see whether Elijah comes to save him!"

Jesus moistened his lips with the sour wine. His work was now accomplished and he was ready to free his spirit. He cried out again in a firm, clear voice:

"It is finished!"

And to his listeners it sounded not like a cry of despair, but a cry of victory.

Now Jesus spoke his last words on the cross. "Father, into your hands I entrust my spirit."

When he had said this, he bowed his head, and died.

At the very moment in which he yielded up his spirit the curtain that veiled the inner sanctuary of the temple in Jerusalem was torn in two from top to bottom. The earth quaked, great rocks shattered; tombs opened, and saints rose from their sleep to leave their graves.

The Roman centurion in charge of the guard saw how Jesus had yielded up his spirit; he saw the earthquake and many other strange and wonderful things that happened in the moment of Jesus' death, and he was so frightened and amazed that he cried out in glory of God. "This surely was a righteous man!" he said in awe. "Truly he must have been a Son of God!" And others echoed him.

But now it was all over. The crowds that had gathered to watch the spectacle turned away, beating their breasts, and went back to the city. But the friends of Jesus, and his mother, and many women who had followed him from Galilee, stayed there watching from a distance. Among them were Mary Magdalene, and Salome the wife of Zebedee and mother of James and John, and Mary the wife of Alphaeus and mother of the other James. All had loved him deeply; and all were overcome with sorrow for their Master and for his weeping mother.

It was now mid-afternoon, and the beginning of the sabbath would come with the setting of the sun. And because the bodies could neither be removed from the crosses or allowed to remain upon them on the sabbath day, least of all during the passover season, the Jews went to Pilate and asked that the bodies be removed at once. Pilate agreed to their request and sent his soldiers back to Calvary.

First they made sure that the two robbers were dead. Then they came to Jesus. They knew he was already dead, yet one of the soldiers thrust a spear into his side; and from the wound there flowed both water and blood. They stared at the limp body in surprise, not knowing that they were fulfilling yet another prophecy: "They shall look upon the man whom they have pierced."

When it was close to evening there came a rich man from Arimathea, named Joseph, who went to see Pilate to ask for the body of Jesus. Now Joseph was a Pharisee and a respected member of the council, but like Nicodemus he was a good and righteous man who had vehemently objected to any suggestion that Jesus might be harmed. In fact, when the council had held their hasty pre-dawn meeting, they had taken good care to exclude both Joseph and Nicodemus. They knew that these two men were sympathetic toward the Nazarene. What they did not know was that both of them were actually disciples of Jesus, and were, themselves, looking for the kingdom of God through the man from Nazareth.

And now Joseph of Arimathea stood boldly before Pilate, asking for the body of Jesus so that he might bury it. Pilate granted permission.

Joseph therefore went to the place of death, taking with him fine linen cloths to wrap around the body. Nicodemus went also, taking a mixture of myrrh and aloes to perfume the grave clothes. Ordinarily the body would be carefully washed and anointed before burial, but there was no time for that. Together the two men took Jesus down from the cross. Together they bound his body in the linen cloths with the spices, in accordance with the Jewish custom. Then, with the help of friends, they gently carried Jesus to a tomb in a garden near the place of the cross.

It was Joseph's own new tomb, one that he had hewn from rock for the day of his own burial, and no man had ever yet been laid in it. Now Joseph was using it as a resting place for Jesus so that the Master might be buried before sundown, and in a place where his body would be safe from enemies who might wish to steal or desecrate it.

The eleven disciples were hiding in Jerusalem. But the women who had come from Galilee followed the small procession and saw Jesus being gently placed within the tomb. Then Joseph rolled a great stone against the mouth of the tomb and departed for his home. When this was done the women left, too, and went off, mourning bitterly. And they rested on the sabbath day, according to the commandment.

The first night of sorrow passed. Very early in the morning the chief priests and Pharisees hurried off to Pilate and made another request. For during the night they had been struck by a thought that had not even occurred to any of the followers of Jesus.

"Sir," they said to Pilate, "we remember that when the deceiver Jesus was alive he said, 'In three days I will rise again.' We ask, therefore, that you give orders to have the tomb closely guarded and secured until the third day. For it may be that his disciples will try to come at night and steal him away, afterwards saying to the people that he has risen from the dead."

"Take the guard," said Pilate. "Make the tomb as secure as you can."

So they went off with the officers and made the grave as secure as they could by sealing the stone and leaving a guard on watch.

This was the second day of Jesus' death.

When the sabbath was over at sunset of that day, Mary Magdalene and Mary the mother of James, and Salome who had followed Jesus through Galilee, went out and bought sweet spices and ointments so that they might properly anoint the body of Jesus whom they loved. When the night had passed and the early morning hours had come, they would go to the tomb and make the burial preparations for which there had been no time before. So the women made plans to go to the garden first thing in the morning.

But the eleven disciples remained behind closed doors, afraid for themselves and full of sorrow over Jesus. They had wanted a king and they had dreamed of glory, and now the dream was gone with the death of Jesus. They had loved him; they had learned much from him; but they had never really understood all he had told them about the nature of the kingdom of God, or what he had meant when he had said that he would rise again. Now they sat there without hope, staring silently at each other and not even thinking to count the days.

The morning of the first day of the new week dawned. It was the third day of the death of Jesus. The Roman soldiers still stood on watch outside the tomb. With the coming of the dawn the ground began to tremble and shake, and a great earthquake racked the garden where Joseph of Arimathea had laid Jesus in the cave. An angel of the Lord came down from heaven and rolled away the stone from the mouth of the tomb, and calmly sat upon it. His face was as bright as lightning, and his raiment as white as dazzling snow; and his watchers gaped and turned pale with fear. They stared at the angel, quaking, and so overcome with shock were they that they fell to the ground like men who had been struck dead.

When they recovered themselves they got up and fled into the city to report what they had seen. They ran very quickly, and they did not look back.

It was very early when Mary Magdalene and the other women came with their spices to anoint their beloved Jesus. The guard had gone, but this did not surprise them for they had not known that any soldiers had been posted. As they walked into the garden they were saying to one another, "Who will roll back for us the stone from the doorway of the tomb?" for the stone was much too heavy for the women to handle alone. Then they reached the tomb. And what they saw then did surprise them.

The stone had already been rolled back from the cave. And when they looked in through the open doorway they saw that the body of Jesus was no longer there.[1]

---

[1]Pearl S. Buck, "The Crucifixion" in *The Story Bible* (New York: Bartholomew House Ltd., 1971), 503–511.

THE DEAL

William Griffin

On the night before Jesus died on the cross, one of his best friends, Judas, told some of his enemies where he would be sleeping. These enemies knew if they could arrest Jesus late at night, there wouldn't be many people around to stand up for him. Judas agreed to tell his enemies where he was for thirty pieces of silver.

Judas looked nervous.

"What seems to be the trouble?" asked the high priest.

"Jesus says one thing, but he does another."

"What do you mean?" asked the high priest.

"He says 'give to the poor' but he himself keeps some of the gifts."

"All the time?"

"Just some of the time."

"Perhaps we should look into this," said the priest.

"It's so discouraging," said Judas.

"We have been wanting to talk to him for some time now."

"I think you should," said Judas.

"But how can we talk to him privately?" asked the priest. "Crowds follow him everywhere he goes."

"I could tell you when he's by himself," said Judas.

"That would be so good," said the priest.

"What's in it for me?" asked Judas.

"What do you have in mind?" asked the priest.

"I was thinking of money."

"How much?"

"Sixty pieces of silver."

"Ten pieces of silver was what we had in mind."

"Fifty, not a piece less."

"I suppose we could offer you twenty, but not a piece more."

"Forty is as low as I'll go."

"Thirty will buy a lot of bread for the poor."

"Sold," said Judas.

"Good," said the priest.

"And have the money ready when I come back," said Judas as he went out to find Jesus.[2]

---

[2]Griffin, "The Deal," 83–84.

THE MYSTERY OF THE CROSS

John Fischer

John Fischer has been one of evangelical America's favorite talents. So much praise attends his reputations. But this retelling of a familiar tale demonstrates he is the friend of children, calling all of them to remember the price Christ paid to make heaven the hope of all children.

∞

I'm sorry to disturb you, Pilate, but there's someone here to see you . . . says he wants to do something with the body."

"What body? Don't you know it's after hours? Send him back tomorrow."

"The body of that Jewish messiah," said the temple guard with the slur of a man who had already started on his happy hour before he left the office. Pilate looked at him with disgust. He would have ripped the man's job out from under him right then and there if he hadn't been one of Caesar's appointments. All of his problems, it seemed to Pilate, were Caesar's appointments.

"I wouldn't have bothered you except that he is a rather prominent man from Arimathea. I'm sure he will make it worth your while," he said, patting his coin belt and pulling back his lips to reveal a Cheshire-cat smile fat with the feathers of its own fresh bribe.

"All right. Bring me my robe and send him in. Wait a minute . . . you aren't talking about that Jesus character, are you? The one we crucified this afternoon?"

"Yes," said the temple guard, as Pilate's personal valet helped him into his robe. "That's the one."

"Impossible. No one dies that quickly on a cross. Have you any confirmation?"

"No, sir."

"Well, I'm certainly not going to give anyone the body of a criminal without confirmation of death. Get me the centurion in charge of today's operation." He waved the guard away.

"Jesus . . . the 'King of the Jews,' " he reminded himself under his breath. "Will I ever be done with this man?"

Pilate adjusted his robe and strolled to the window while the footsteps of the guard disappeared down the hall. It seemed to him that the sun went down early on this day. It was one day he would just as soon forget anyway. He wondered why it felt like the middle of the night.

"Gaius," he said to his valet, "what time is it?"

"It's time to close the office, sir."

"But why is it so dark?"

"It's been this way since the middle of the afternoon, sir. I don't know why. Nothing but dark clouds without rain."

Suddenly a centurion guard appeared at the entrance to the room.

"How did you get here so fast? Why aren't you at the site? What's going on here? Am I the only person who knows it's not the middle of the night?"

"Sir, we left the site an hour ago. I gave most of the men the night off. We broke the legs of two of them. They'll scream all night. Strangest thing, though. The other one is already dead."

"The Jew?"

"Yes, sir."

"Will you vouch for that?"

"Sir, I personally shoved my spear right up to his heart. He was dead. No breath. No movement. Strangest thing: Blood and water came out. Never saw that before."

"Blood and water?" Pilate walked back to the window and thought. Lots of things were happening today that people had never seen before. What was going on?

"How many guards are there now?"

"Two, sir. The crowd has fairly dispersed. Only a couple of women crying over the dead one."

"Very well. You may go. Guard, bring me Mr. Fat Belt from Arimathea."

The temple guard flashed his toothy smile again, but Pilate only stared at him.

"Thank you, Your Honor, for seeing me after hours," Joseph said nervously as he hurried into the room. "I am prepared to make it worth—"

"No need. I have already washed my hands of this matter, and I do not wish to dirty them again. What is it you want?"

"We would like the body of Jesus of Nazareth for burial. I have a tomb on my property already prepared."

"Why tonight? He can come down tomorrow with the others."

"Your Honor, if you would, please. Our custom is that no work be done on the Sabbath. Today is our Day of Preparation. I have made all the proper arrangements. I will take care of everything."

Pilate looked at Joseph's clothes and wondered what interest a well-to-do businessman would have in a poor country preacher whose luck had obviously run out.

"Are you related to him?"

Joseph hesitated and then surprised himself with what on the one hand was a lie but on the other was the most certain truth he had ever spoken.

"Yes."

"All right. You may have your dead man, but you will have two guards with you to ensure that the body gets put in that tomb and sealed properly. Guard, fetch me the centurion again!"

⋘►‖◄⋙

Pilate sent Joseph and the head centurion away, hoping to be finally done with the ordeal. He had a strong urge to wash his hands again but ignored it. "Leave me alone for a few minutes," he said to Gaius, and he slumped down into his chair, rubbing his eyes. Suddenly the memory of Jesus standing before him only hours before sprang to his mind, and he heard every word again.

"Are you the king of the Jews?"

"Is that your own idea, or did others talk to you about me?" The audacity of this man, speaking to him like that! Pilate had wanted to strike him, but something constrained him. That strange warning message from his wife, the dreams . . .

Pilate did remember reacting to Jesus by saying, "Am I a Jew?" He liked that. It was a smart thing to have said, he thought. Almost as smart as when he deposited his brilliant question: "What is truth?" and then left without an answer.

"It was your people and your chief priests who handed you over to me. What is it you have done, anyway?"

"My kingdom is not of this world." Pilate recalled the prisoner's words, and as he sat at his desk and reviewed the events of this strange day, he had to admit that he almost believed the man. What kind of king would find himself in his hour of need abandoned by all his followers? If he was a king, it certainly wasn't of any place in or around Pilate's jurisdiction.

Pilate was more than prepared to cross Jesus off as just another nut case—and that is, indeed, what he would do. God knows he'd seen enough of them in his rule. But that was just the problem. He'd seen too many nut cases—too many to be able to pass this one off as just one more. If this man was crazy, he was crazy in a most intelligent way, for Pilate had never heard anyone speak this way before. This man was too smart. There was something different about him—something that made Pilate almost believe it when he said he was from some other world.

"My kingdom is not of this world." Pilate muttered the words to himself, and suddenly he imagined Joseph pulling the dead body of the king of the Jews down from the cross. He chuckled lightly. His kingdom was sure enough not of this world anymore. His followers had seen to that.[3]

---

[3]John Fischer, "The Mystery of the Cross" in *On a Hill Too Far Away* (Minneapolis: Bethany House, 2001), 43–46, 50–52.

RAGMAN

Walter Wangerin

*In this story Jesus is portrayed as a ragman, who
befriends the hurting people of the inner city.
Walter Wangerin is one of Christianity's favorite
writers. This story shows how Jesus made our lives
easier by making his own a matter of
sacrifice and pain.*

❧

I saw a strange sight. I stumbled upon a story most strange, like nothing my life, my street sense, my sly tongue had ever prepared me for.

Hush, child. Hush, now, and I will tell it to you.

Even before the dawn one Friday morning I noticed a young man, handsome and strong, walking the alleys of our city. He was pulling an old cart filled with clothes both bright and new, and he was calling in a clear, tenor voice: "Rags!" Ah, the air was foul and the first light filthy to be crossed by such sweet music.

"Rags! New rags for old! I take your tired rags! Rags!"

"Now, this is a wonder," I thought to myself, for the man stood six-feet-four, and his arms were like tree limbs, hard and muscular, and his eyes flashed intelligence. Could he find no better job than this, to be a ragman in the inner city?

I followed him. My curiosity drove me. And I wasn't disappointed.

Soon the Ragman saw a woman sitting on her back porch. She was sobbing into a handkerchief, sighing, and shedding a thousand tears. Her knees and elbows made a sad X. Her shoulders shook. Her heart was breaking.

The Ragman stopped his cart. Quietly, he walked to the woman, stepping round tin cans, dead toys, and Pampers.

"Give me your rag," he said so gently, "and I'll give you another."

He slipped the handkerchief from her eyes. She looked up, and he laid across her palm a linen cloth so clean and new that it shined. She blinked from the gift to the giver. Then, as he began to pull his cart again, the Ragman did a strange thing: he put her stained handkerchief to his own face; and then *he* began to weep, to sob as grievously as she had done, his shoulders shaking. Yet she was left without a tear.

"This *is* a wonder," I breathed to myself, and I followed the sobbing Ragman like a child who cannot turn away from mystery.

"Rags! Rags! New rags for old!"

In a little while, when the sky showed grey behind the rooftops and I could see the shredded curtains hanging out black windows, the Ragman came upon a girl whose head was wrapped in a bandage, whose eyes were empty. Blood soaked her bandage. A single line of blood ran down her cheek.

Now the tall Ragman looked upon this child with pity, and he drew a lovely yellow bonnet from his cart.

"Give me your rag," he said, tracing his own line on her cheek, "and I'll give you mine."

The child could only gaze at him while he loosened the bandage, removed it, and tied it to his own head. The bonnet he set on hers. And I gasped at what I saw: for with the bandage went the wound! Against his brow it ran a darker, more substantial blood—his own!

"Rags! Rags! I take old rags!" cried the sobbing, bleeding, strong, intelligent Ragman.

The sun hurt both the sky, now, and my eyes; the Ragman seemed more and more to hurry.

"Are you going to work?" he asked a man who leaned against a telephone pole. The man shook his head.

The Ragman pressed him: "Do you have a job?"

"Are you crazy?" sneered the other. He pulled away from the pole, revealing the right sleeve of his jacket—flat, the cuff stuffed into the pocket. He had no arm.

"So," said the Ragman. "Give me your jacket, and I'll give you mine."

Such quiet authority in his voice!

The one-armed man took off his jacket. So did the Ragman—and I trembled at what I saw: for the Ragman's arm stayed in its sleeve, and when the other put it on he had two good arms, thick as tree limbs; but the Ragman had only one.

"Go to work," he said.

After that he found a drunk, lying unconscious beneath an army blanket, an old man, hunched, wizened, and sick. He took that blanket and wrapped it round himself, but for the drunk he left new clothes.

And now I had to run to keep up with the Ragman. Though he was weeping uncontrollably, and bleeding freely at the forehead, pulling his cart with one arm, stumbling for drunkenness, falling again and again, exhausted, old, and sick, yet he went with terrible speed. On spider's legs he skittered through the alleys of the City, this mile and the next, until he came to its limits, and then he rushed beyond.

I wept to see the change in this man. I hurt to see his sorrow. And yet I needed to see where he was going in such haste, perhaps to know what drove him so.

The little old Ragman—he came to a landfill. He came to the garbage pits. And then I wanted to help him in what he did, but I hung back, hiding. He climbed a hill. With tormented labor he cleared a little space on that hill. Then he sighed. He lay down. He pillowed his head on a handkerchief and a jacket. He covered his bones with an army blanket. And he died.

Oh, how I cried to witness that death! I slumped in a junked car and wailed and mourned as one who has no hope—because I had come to love the Ragman. Every other face had faded in the wonder of this man, and I cherished him; but he died. I sobbed myself to sleep.

I did not know—how could I know?—that I slept through Friday night and Saturday and its night, too.

But then, on Sunday morning, I was wakened by a violence.

Light—pure, hard, demanding light—slammed against my sour face, and I blinked, and I looked, and I saw the last and the first wonder of all. There was the Ragman, folding the blanket most carefully, a scar on his forehead, but alive! And besides that, healthy! There was no sign of sorrow nor of age, and all the rags that he had gathered shined for cleanliness.

Well, then I lowered my head and, trembling for all that I had seen, I myself walked up to the Ragman. I told him my name with shame, for I was a sorry figure next to him. Then I took off all my clothes in that place, and I said to him with dear yearning in my voice: "Dress me."

He dressed me. My Lord, he put new rags on me, and I am a wonder beside him. The Ragman, the Ragman, the Christ![4]

---

[4]Walter Wangerin, "Ragman" in *Ragman and Other Cries of Faith* (San Francisco: Harper & Row, 1984), 3–6.

"THE TRIUMPH OF LIFE"
RICHARD STERGULZ

CHAPTER SEVEN

THE

BIG

SURPRISE

ON THE THIRD DAY
HE WILL BE RAISED TO LIFE!
MATTHEW 20:19B (NIV)

Have you ever considered the world's greatest discoverers? Marco Polo discovered an overland route to China. Christopher Columbus discovered America. Ferdinand Magellan discovered the Pacific Ocean. Jonas Salk discovered a cure for polio. Louis Pasteur discovered a way to make milk safe to drink. But none of these discoveries, as wonderful as they were, were the world's greatest discovery.

This—the greatest of all discoveries—was made by a woman named Mary Magdalene. She went to Jesus' grave to take some burial spices to put on his dead body so it wouldn't smell so bad. When she got there, she found that the huge stone that had been rolled over the mouth of the tomb had been rolled away. Not only that, but the body of her dead friend Jesus was no longer in the tomb where it had been put after it was taken down from the cross. Mary was really upset because she felt that some grave robbers had come and stolen Jesus' body. Then Jesus himself appeared to her.

Jesus was too kind to say, "I'm baaaack! Mary, you ought to be ashamed that you do not recognize me." In fact, Jesus said nothing at all. He just stood there.

Mary wasn't thinking straight, and she thought Jesus was the gardener. It was pretty early in the morning before daylight, so we mustn't be too hard on her for the mistake. Imagine her excitement when Jesus called her name. She became so excited that she clung to him in real affection. Jesus told her not to cling to him, and she let him go. Then Jesus told her to go and tell his friends that he was alive.

She did. She ran into their presence and said something like, "Surprise! Guess who's not dead anymore!"

They were all overjoyed. Then that very night Jesus appeared to ten of his friends at once. They were all present except for Thomas. Believe me, they were so happy they were laughing and whooping their joy. Later, when they tried to tell Thomas that they had all seen Jesus alive, Thomas said, "You guys made that up!"

There's one in nearly every crowd: one who doubts when everyone else believes. Usually they write books on how senseless such ideas as resurrection are. They tried and tried to tell him it was true, but Thomas remained unconvinced. He thought they had all been too long in the sun and were having a joint delusion of some sort. It is for that reason that we still call him Doubting Thomas. Thomas really did more than say, "I doubt that." What he really said—at least in his demeanor—was, "Not a chance. I watched him die on Friday. They even ran a spear in his side to make sure he was dead. Nope! He cannot possibly be alive. There are a lot of statistics on this sort of thing, you know. One hundred percent of dead people keep on being dead. You guys must think I was born yesterday." All of a sudden he was getting pretty loud in declaring his doubts: "Unless I myself see him alive and run my finger in the nail holes in his hands and thrust my hand into the huge hole made in his side by the spear, I will never believe."

Most of the apostles thought Thomas was overdoing his doubts a little.

The next week Thomas was with the rest of the disciples when . . . *poof!* Jesus showed up again. "Thomas," he said, "here, put your fingers in these nail prints and run your hand into the hole in my side."

Boy! Was Thomas embarrassed. He looked at Jesus' hands. They were so torn that Thomas was too humiliated to put his finger in the nail holes. He just bowed his head and fell on his knees and said, "My Lord and my God!" When he first lifted his eyes, he saw one of his friends wagging his finger and smiling. While he said nothing out loud, he shot Thomas a glance that seemed to say, "Tsk, tsk! We told you so!"

After he rose from the dead, Jesus hung around Jerusalem and Galilee for about six weeks. He appeared to all of his friends several times. Then finally, when they were all convinced that he really was alive, he took them to a mountain called Olivet. From there he ascended. He just rose up from the top of that hill and kept on rising. They watched him as long as they could see him, until his body was just a tiny speck of white against the deep blue of the sky. Then he disappeared, and they knew that he was gone and that they wouldn't be seeing him for a long time.

But even as he disappeared, two men—probably angels—who were dressed in shining white garments said to them, "You people of Galilee. There is no need for you to keep on looking up. He is truly gone. Rubbing your eyes to try to get a final glimpse of him will not avail. He is gone, but not forever. Even as you have seen him go up into heaven, someday he will come back again."

Now Christians everywhere keep looking for him to come back. Nobody knows when that will happen. Here and there, someone will say, "Oh, that will never happen." Personally, I wouldn't ever say that. Thomas tried to deny that he had come back alive, and look how wrong he was. It's better not to doubt the angels. So far no angel has ever been wrong.

THE RESURRECTION

Charles Dickens

Jesus could be killed, but he couldn't
be held by death.

✐

When that morning began to dawn, Mary Magdalene and the other Mary and some other women, came to the sepulchre, with some more spices which they had prepared. As they were saying to each other, "How shall we roll away the stone?" the earth trembled and shook, and an Angel, descending from Heaven, rolled it back, and then sat resting on it. His countenance was like lightning, and his garments were white as snow; and at sight of him the men of the guard fainted away with fear, as if they were dead.

Mary Magdalene saw the stone rolled away, and waiting to see no more, ran to Peter and John who were coming towards the place, and said, "they have taken away the Lord and we know not where they have laid Him!" They immediately ran to the tomb, but John, being the faster of the two, outran the other, and got there first. He stooped down, and looked in, and saw the linen clothes in which the body had been wrapped, lying there; but he did not go in. When Peter came up, he went in, and saw the linen clothes lying in one place, and a napkin that had been bound about the head, in another. John also went in, then, and saw the same things. Then they went home, to tell the rest.

But Mary Magdalene remained outside the sepulchre, weeping. After a little time, she stooped down, and looked in, and saw two Angels, clothed in white, sitting where the body of Christ had lain. These said to her, "Woman, why weepest thou?" She answered, "Because they have taken away my Lord, and I know not where they have laid Him." As she gave this answer, she turned round, and saw Jesus standing behind her, but did not then know Him. "Woman," said He, "why weepest thou? What seekest thou?" She, supposing Him to be the gardener, replied, "Sir! If thou hast borne my Lord hence, tell me where thou hast laid Him, and I will take Him away." Jesus pronounced her name, "Mary." Then she knew Him, and, starting, exclaimed, "Master!"—"Touch me not," said Christ; "for I am not yet ascended to my Father; but go to my Disciples, and say unto them, I ascend unto my Father; and your Father; and to my God and to your God!"

Accordingly, Mary Magdalene went and told the Disciples that she had seen Christ, and what He had said to her; and with them she found the other women whom she had left at the sepulchre when she had gone to call those two Disciples, Peter and John. These women told her and the rest, that they had seen at the tomb, two men in shining garments at sight of whom they had been afraid, and had bent down, but who had told them that the Lord was risen; and also that as they came to tell this, they had seen Christ, on the way, and had held him by the feet, and worshipped Him. But these accounts seemed to the Apostles, at that time, as idle tales, and they did not believe them.

The soldiers of the guard too, when they recovered from their fainting-fit, and went to the chief priests to tell them what they had seen, were silenced with large sums of money, and were told by them to say that the Disciples had stolen the body away while they were asleep.

But it happened that on that same day, Simon and Cleopas—Simon one of the twelve Apostles, and Cleopas one of the followers of Christ—were walking to a village called Emmaus, at some little distance from Jerusalem, and were talking, by the way, upon the death and resurrection of Christ, when they were joined by a stranger, who explained the Scriptures to them, and told them a great deal about God, so that they wondered at His knowledge. As the night was fast coming on when they reached the village, they asked this stranger to stay with them, which He consented to do. When they all three sat down to supper, He took some bread, and blessed it, and broke it as Christ had done at the Last Supper. Looking on Him in wonder they found that His face was changed before them, and that it was Christ Himself; and as they looked on Him, He disappeared.

They instantly rose up, and returned to Jerusalem, and finding the Disciples sitting together, told them what they had seen. While they were speaking, Jesus suddenly stood in the midst of all the company, and said, "Peace be unto ye!" Seeing that they were greatly frightened, He showed them His hands and feet, and invited them to touch

Him; and, to encourage them and give them time to recover themselves, He ate a piece of broiled fish and a piece of honeycomb before them all.

But Thomas, one of the twelve Apostles, was not there, at that time; and when the rest said to him afterwards, "We have seen the Lord!" he answered, "Except I shall see in His hands the print of the nails, and thrust my hand into His side, I will not believe!" At that moment, though the doors were all shut, Jesus again appeared, standing among them, and said, "Peace be unto you!" Then He said to Thomas, "Reach hither thy finger, and behold my hands; and reach hither thy hand, and thrust it into my side; and be not faithless, but believing." And Thomas answered, and said to Him, "My Lord and my God!" Then said Jesus, "Thomas, because thou hast seen me, thou hast believed. Blessed are they that have not seen me, and yet have believed."

After that time, Jesus Christ was seen by five hundred of His followers at once, and He remained with others of them forty days, teaching them, and instructing them to go forth into the world, and preach His gospel and religion: not minding what wicked men might do to them. And conducting His Disciples at last out of Jerusalem as far as Bethany, He blessed them, and ascended in a cloud to Heaven, and took His place at the right hand of God. And while they gazed into the bright blue sky where He had vanished, two white-robed Angels appeared among them, and told them that as they had seen Christ ascend to Heaven, so He would, one day, come descending from it, to judge the world.[1]

---

[1]Dickens, "The Death," 111–121.

JESUS APPEARS TO HIS FOLLOWERS AND THOMAS

John 20:19–29 (ICB)

''Seeing is believing'' is an old proverb. But in this passage Jesus reverses the order and says that if you're willing to believe what you can't see, your inner sight will come alive with truth that only the heart can see. It is, after all, inner sight which matters most.

☙

It was the first day of the week. That evening the followers were together. The doors were locked, because they were afraid of the Jews. Then Jesus came and stood among them. He said, "Peace be with you!" After he said this, he showed them his hands and his side. The followers were very happy when they saw the Lord.

Then Jesus said again, "Peace be with you! As the Father sent me, I now send you." After he said this, he breathed on them and said, "Receive the Holy Spirit. If you forgive anyone his sins, they are forgiven. If you don't forgive them, they are not forgiven."

Thomas (called Didymus) was not with the followers when Jesus came. Thomas was one of the twelve. The other followers told Thomas, "We saw the Lord."

But Thomas said, "I will not believe it until I see the nail marks in his hands. And I will not believe until I put my finger where the nails were and put my hand into his side."

A week later the followers were in the house again. Thomas was with them. The doors were locked, but Jesus came in and stood among them. He said, "Peace be with you!" Then he said to Thomas, "Put your finger here. Look at my hands. Put your hand here in my side. Stop doubting and believe."

Thomas said to him, "My Lord and my God!"

Then Jesus told him, "You believe because you see me. Those who believe without seeing me will be truly happy."

THE ONE MINUTE LIFE OF CHRIST

Calvin Miller

*Christ's life was simple, and yet it was
the greatest life ever lived.*

Joseph the carpenter
Early one morn
God married to Mary
And Jesus was born—
Though God and not Joseph
Was really his father.
Joseph loved Jesus
And so did his mother.

Then Jesus grew up
And was baptized by John,
Who wore camel's hair
And ate bugs and honey.
Yuck! He didn't care
If his breath was so bad
It colored the air,
'Cause John sure loved God
As anyone must
If he says his grace proper
Before he sits down
To a plate of grasshoppers.

Then Jesus went down
To the shore of the sea
And saw Jim and Johnny
Bar Zebedee.
He said, "Follow me,"
And they did—as did others
Like Peter and Andrew,
Who also were brothers.
Eight more soon followed—
One dozen in all—
Round, squat and fat ones,
Thin, skinny, and tall.
Simon was dense,
And Thomas intense,
And Judas Iscariot
Straddled the fence.

For three years Christ traveled
Around with his friends
Till Herod and Pilate
Said, "This is the end!"

They hung our dear Lord
On a cross in the sky—
He gave up his life—
It made Mary cry.

They thought he was dead,
But their faces grew red
When he got out of bed
And walked from the tomb
As the lightning went "pow"
And the thunder "kaboom."
But soon he ascended
(That means to arise
And float up and away
Beyond the blue skies.)

But down came the Spirit
That first Pentecost!
His friends started preaching
To act out his Way.
This news spread like wildfire:
"He's home with his father,
But there he won't stay.
He'll come back some day—
He's gone until then,
But he's coming again!"

This news was so joyous—
So splendid, so grand—
Christianity spread
All over the land.[2]

---

[2]Calvin Miller, "The One Minute Life of Christ" in *Apples, Snakes and Bellyaches* (Dallas: Word Publishing, 1990), 131–135.

THE REST
OF THE STORY

Tricia McCary Rhodes

*Tricia McCary Rhodes reminds children of all ages
that the most redeeming and treasured phrase stands
at the heart of our faith. Those three words are
"Christ Is Risen." These three words launched
Jesus' grieving friends into a new world of joy.
When God brought Jesus back to life, the very idea
that death was dark and terminal was done with.
Jesus proved that death is only an illusion.
It is life, which is real.*

*Just as Jesus put death in its place, we too shall
show this dark threat that the tomb of Christ is
open and empty. He is alive. As the hymn
writer put it:*

> Death could not keep his prey
> Jesus my Savior
> He tore the bars away
> Jesus my Lord.

*We were made to live forever. Jesus showed us that
we will do it. Hallelujah!*

❧

When the last of Saturday's sun sinks below the horizon, the long Sabbath ends, propelling the women into action. Three go to purchase more supplies while the marketplace is still open. Upon their return, tender hands crush and mix dried flowers and pungent spices for hours, all of them soberly sharing this final act of compassion.

When morning nears, they hurry off to the tomb. After walking some distance, one of the women suggests they will have trouble rolling away the stone from the grave, and a discussion ensues concerning whether they should get one of the men. But they are almost there, and no one wants to turn back now.

In the predawn darkness, soldiers stand and stretch, tired from the long night. As the morning watch moves into position, the ground begins to shake under their feet. In astonishment the guards see a dazzling creature descending from heaven. With a face like lightning and clothed in brilliant white, the angel rolls the stone away, taking a seat at the top.

In an instant the guards faint as though dead. Within a few seconds they awake, rushing frantically into the tomb. Panic grips them as they see no trace of a body. The entire group races back toward Jerusalem, terrified at what they have seen, dreading Pilate's response.

The sun creeps across the eastern sky, though the tomb is still shrouded in darkness as the women arrive. Astounded that the stone is removed from the sepulcher's entrance, two of them go inside, shocked at what they see. The body of Jesus is not there.

Suddenly the cave is bathed in light and two men in shining robes dazzle the women. Falling in fear to the ground, the words they hear stun them.

"Why are you looking in a tomb for someone who is alive? He is not here—he is risen! Don't you remember what he said—that the Messiah must be betrayed by evil men and be crucified, and that he would rise again on the third day?"

The women glance at each other, then burst from the cave. Followed by the others, they run back to Jerusalem, where the disciples continue to mourn. Breathless, they tell the men what they have just seen.

The disciples look at them as if they are crazy, dismissing their words as superstitious nonsense. Blinded by grief, each man returns to his unique brand of hopelessness.

Mary Magdalene cannot believe their response. She pleads with Peter and John to believe her. "They have taken the Lord's body—it is gone, and I don't know where they have placed it."

Something in her voice stirs them. They hurry from the house, through the streets of the city to the tomb of Joseph of Arimathea. John, being younger and faster, arrives first. He bends down and sees the empty cloths, but stays back, afraid. Peter catches up quickly and crashes into the cave, determined to find the truth.

There on the stone bench lie the linen cloths, completely undisturbed, as if the body simply disappeared within the folds. On the side lies the headpiece in a tidy roll. Slowly, faith begins to fill the crevices of Peter's broken heart.

John cautiously enters the cave and together they share a moment of pure incredulity. Words from the past echo through their minds. The Rabbi had told them he would rise again—could it be? Is it possible? Can they dare hope? Thoughtfully they walk in silence back to town.

Mary Magdalene, having followed them to the tomb, watches them leave. She begins to weep, stooping down one more time to see the empty grave. But it isn't empty. On either end of the bench, where she'd seen them lay the body of Christ, are two white-robed angels.

"Why do you cry?" one asks.

"Because they've taken my Lord away, and I don't know where they put him."

Sobbing by now, Mary hears a sound behind her. She looks over her shoulder, and the sight of a gardener gives her a glimmer of hope. "Sir, please—if you have taken him away, just tell me where, and I will go and get him."

"Mary."

She freezes. Only one person has ever spoken her name like that before. Long ago, when tortured by demons, Jesus of Nazareth called her "Mary" and set her free. The scene flashes through her mind as she turns to face the one who speaks.

"Master!" Mary exclaims, rushing toward him.

"Wait, Mary, you cannot cling to me now for I haven't yet ascended to my Father. You must go and find my brothers. Tell them that I ascend to my Father and your Father, my God and your God."

Then he is gone. Mary stands for a moment in complete amazement at what she has seen and heard. Tears stream down her cheeks as she goes to the disciples. One by one and in small groups she comes upon those who once walked with Christ.

"*I have seen the Lord*," she tells them. The look in her eyes and wonder in her voice leave no room for doubt that, indeed, she has encountered the risen Christ.

I have seen the Lord. Resurrection hope is spawned in that moment, then spreads like a soothing ointment to those who will believe—some having seen, and others simply by faith—that what Jesus of Nazareth said he would do, he did. And resurrection hope transcends time, instilling eternity in the hearts of mankind.[3]

[3]Tricia McCary Rhodes, "The Rest of the Story" in *Contemplating the Cross* (Minneapolis: Bethany House, 1998), 181–184.

CHRIST THE LORD IS RISEN TODAY

Charles Wesley

Charles Wesley, the brother of the famed evangelist John Wesley, wrote many songs, but none resounds with Christianity's greatest truth more than this one. Christ the Lord is risen today, yet every day his continuing life adorns the life of his church. Raise your joys and triumphs high? Why? Christ has opened paradise! He lives! We live! Forever! Hallelujah!

Christ the Lord is risen today,
  Alleluia!
Sons of men and angels say.
  Alleluia!
Raise your joys and triumphs high;
  Alleluia!
Sing, ye heavens, and earth reply:
  Alleluia!

Love's redeeming work is done,
  Alleluia!
Fought the fight, the battle won;
  Alleluia!
Death in vain forbids Him rise,

Alleluia!
Christ has opened Paradise.
Alleluia!

Lives again our glorious King;
Alleluia!
Where, O death, is now thy sting?
Alleluia!
Dying once, He all doth save:
Alleluia!
Where's thy victory, O grave?
Alleluia!

Soar we now where Christ has led,
Alleluia!
Following our exalted Head;
Alleluia!
Made like Him, like Him we rise;
Alleluia!
Ours the cross, the grave, the skies.
Alleluia![4]

---

[4]Charles Wesley, "Christ the Lord Is Risen Today" in *Lyra Davidica* (London: 1708).